A Midsummer Night's Dream

and Related Readings

McDougal Littell
A HOUGHTON MIFFLIN COMPANY
Evanston, Illinois   *Boston*   *Dallas*

Acknowledgments

Viking Penguin: Excerpt from *The Friendly Shakespeare* by Norrie Epstein. Copyright © 1993 by Norrie Epstein, Jon Winokur, and Reid Boates. Used by permission of Viking Penguin, a division of Penguin Books USA Inc.

University of Pennsylvania Press: "The Sweet Miracle" by Juana de Ibarbourou, from *Some Spanish-American Poets*, edited and translated by Alice Stone Blackwell. Copyright 1929 by Alice Stone Blackwell. Reprinted with permission from the University of Pennsylvania Press.

Don Congdon Associates, Inc.: "The April Witch" by Ray Bradbury, first appeared in the *Saturday Evening Post*. Copyright © 1952, renewed 1980 by Ray Bradbury. Reprinted by permission of Don Congdon Associates, Inc.

Random House, Inc.: "Come. And Be My Baby," from *Oh Pray My Wings Are Gonna Fit Me Well* by Maya Angelou. Copyright © 1975 by Maya Angelou. Reprinted by permission of Random House, Inc.

Continued on page 223.

The editors have made every effort to trace the ownership of all copyrighted selections found in this book and to make full acknowledgment for their use. Omissions brought to our attention will be corrected in a subsequent edition.

Cover illustration by Curtis Parker.
Author picture: North Wind Picture Archives.

ISBN 0-395-77543-4

2003 Impression.
Copyright © 1997 by McDougal Littell Inc. All rights reserved. Printed in the United States of America.

8 9 10 11 QVK 05 04 03

Contents

A Midsummer Night's Dream

William Shakespeare

Characters

FOUR LOVERS

Hermia

Lysander

Helena

Demetrius

Theseus, duke of Athens

Hippolyta, queen of the Amazons

Egeus, father to Hermia

Philostrate, master of the revels to Theseus

Nick Bottom, weaver

Peter Quince, carpenter

Francis Flute, bellows-mender

Tom Snout, tinker

Snug, joiner

Robin Starveling, tailor

Oberon, king of the Fairies

Titania, queen of the Fairies

Robin Goodfellow, a "puck," or hobgoblin, in Oberon's
service

A Fairy, in the service of Titania

FAIRIES ATTENDING UPON TITANIA

Peaseblossom

Cobweb

Mote

Mustardseed

Lords and Attendants on Theseus and Hippolyta

Other Fairies in the trains of Titania and Oberon

1-2 *our nuptial . . . apace:* The time of our wedding quickly approaches.

4-6 Theseus compares the old moon, which delays his marriage by lingering, to a stepmother or widow who delays or diminishes a young man's inheritance while she remains alive.

7 *steep:* soak.

ACT ONE

Scene 1 *The palace of Theseus in Athens.*

Theseus, the Duke of Athens, can hardly wait for the next new moon, when he will marry Hippolyta, Queen of the Amazons. Their wedding preparations are interrupted by the arrival of Egeus, his daughter Hermia, and her two suitors. Hermia wishes to marry Lysander, but Egeus has given his consent to Demetrius. Hermia refuses to marry Demetrius, who recently courted and then abandoned her friend Helena. Egeus insists on a harsh punishment. Theseus reluctantly agrees that if Hermia disobeys her father she must face the Athenian penalty—either death or a life of chastity. He gives her four days to decide. Alone, Lysander and Hermia make plans to meet in the woods the next night and escape to his aunt's house, where they will be safe from Athenian law. When Helena appears, still heartbroken over her loss of Demetrius, they tell her about their planned elopement. She decides to betray their plans to Demetrius in hope of regaining his favor.

[Enter Theseus, Hippolyta, and Philostrate, with others.]

Theseus. Now, fair Hippolyta, our nuptial hour
　　Draws on apace. Four happy days bring in
　　Another moon. But, O, methinks how slow
　　This old moon wanes! She lingers my desires
5　　Like to a stepdame or a dowager
　　Long withering out a young man's revenue.

Hippolyta. Four days will quickly steep themselves in night;
　　Four nights will quickly dream away the time;

11 *solemnities:* wedding ceremony.

13 *pert:* lively.

14–15 Theseus says that melancholy, that pale fellow, is
appropriate for funerals but not for his festive parade.

16–17 According to the stories of mythology, Theseus
defeated Hippolyta and her fellow Amazons, a race of
female warriors.

19 *triumph:* public festivity.

31 *With feigning voice:* in a soft voice; ***feigning love:***
pretended love.

32–34 Lysander has stolen his way into Hermia's heart with
gifts such as playthings ***(gauds),*** fancy articles
(conceits), knickknacks ***(Knacks),*** flower bouquets
(nosegays), and candy ***(sweetmeats).***

35 *prevailment:* influence.

And then the moon, like to a silver bow
10 New-bent in heaven, shall behold the night
Of our solemnities.

Theseus.   Go, Philostrate,
Stir up the Athenian youth to merriments.
Awake the pert and nimble spirit of mirth.
Turn melancholy forth to funerals;
15 The pale companion is not for our pomp.

[Philostrate *exits.*]

Hippolyta, I wooed thee with my sword
And won thy love doing thee injuries,
But I will wed thee in another key,
With pomp, with triumph, and with reveling.

[Enter Egeus *and his daughter* Hermia, *and* Lysander *and*
Demetrius.]

20 **Egeus.** Happy be Theseus, our renownèd duke!

Theseus. Thanks, good Egeus. What's the news with
thee?

Egeus. Full of vexation come I, with complaint
Against my child, my daughter Hermia.—
Stand forth, Demetrius.—My noble lord,
25 This man hath my consent to marry her.—
Stand forth, Lysander.—And, my gracious duke,
This man hath bewitched the bosom of my child.—
Thou, thou, Lysander, thou hast given her rhymes
And interchanged love tokens with my child.
30 Thou hast by moonlight at her window sung
With feigning voice verses of feigning love
And stol'n the impression of her fantasy
With bracelets of thy hair, rings, gauds, conceits,
Knacks, trifles, nosegays, sweetmeats—messengers
35 Of strong prevailment in unhardened youth.
With cunning hast thou filched my daughter's heart,
Turned her obedience (which is due to me)
To stubborn harshness.—And, my gracious duke,

39 *Be it so:* if.

43 *this gentleman:* Demetrius.

45 **Immediately:** directly, without reprieve.

49–51 Theseus compares Hermia to a wax figure that has been created by her father. Egeus has the right to leave that figure alone *(leave)* or to destroy **(disfigure)** it. *What does Theseus's comparison suggest about the rights of women in Athenian society?*

54–55 *But . . . worthier:* Since Lysander lacks her father's approval *(voice),* Demetrius must be considered worthier in this respect.

60 *how it . . . modesty:* whether it is proper behavior.

65–78 If Hermia disobeys her father, she must either be put to death or renounce male companionship. Theseus asks her to consider her youth and passions *(blood)* when deciding whether she could endure living cooped up **(mewed)** in a cloister forever **(For aye),** wearing the clothing *(livery)* of a nun. She would be a virgin **(a**

Be it so she will not here before your Grace
40 Consent to marry with Demetrius,
I beg the ancient privilege of Athens:
As she is mine, I may dispose of her,
Which shall be either to this gentleman
Or to her death, according to our law
45 Immediately provided in that case.

Theseus. What say you, Hermia? Be advised, fair maid.
To you, your father should be as a god,
One that composed your beauties, yea, and one
To whom you are but as a form in wax
50 By him imprinted, and within his power
To leave the figure or disfigure it.
Demetrius is a worthy gentleman.

Hermia. So is Lysander.

Theseus.   In himself he is,
But in this kind, wanting your father's voice,
55 The other must be held the worthier.

Hermia. I would my father looked but with my eyes.

Theseus. Rather your eyes must with his judgment look.

Hermia. I do entreat your Grace to pardon me.
I know not by what power I am made bold,
60 Nor how it may concern my modesty
In such a presence here to plead my thoughts;
But I beseech your Grace that I may know
The worst that may befall me in this case
If I refuse to wed Demetrius.

65 **Theseus.** Either to die the death, or to abjure
Forever the society of men.
Therefore, fair Hermia, question your desires,
Know of your youth, examine well your blood,
Whether (if you yield not to your father's choice)
70 You can endure the livery of a nun,
For aye to be in shady cloister mewed,

barren sister) living in the service of Diana, the goddess of the moon and virginity. Theseus says that although those who control their passions and live as virgins are thrice-blessed, those who marry are happier in this world. (In his metaphor, the married woman is a rose plucked and distilled into perfume.)

80 *my virgin patent:* my right to remain a virgin.

88 *as he would:* as Egeus wishes.

89 *protest:* vow.

90 *austerity:* self-denial.

92 *crazèd title:* flawed claim.

94 *Do you:* you.

98 *estate unto:* give to.

99–100 Lysander says he is as well born and as wealthy as Demetrius.

101 *fairly:* handsomely.

102 *If not with vantage:* if not better.

105 *prosecute:* pursue.

To live a barren sister all your life,
Chanting faint hymns to the cold fruitless moon.
Thrice-blessèd they that master so their blood
75 To undergo such maiden pilgrimage,
But earthlier happy is the rose distilled
Than that which, withering on the virgin thorn,
Grows, lives, and dies in single blessedness.

Hermia. So will I grow, so live, so die, my lord,
80 Ere I will yield my virgin patent up
Unto his lordship whose unwishèd yoke
My soul consents not to give sovereignty.

Theseus. Take time to pause, and by the next new moon
(The sealing day betwixt my love and me
85 For everlasting bond of fellowship),
Upon that day either prepare to die
For disobedience to your father's will,
Or else to wed Demetrius, as he would,
Or on Diana's altar to protest
90 For aye austerity and single life.

Demetrius. Relent, sweet Hermia, and, Lysander, yield
Thy crazèd title to my certain right.

Lysander. You have her father's love, Demetrius.
Let me have Hermia's. Do you marry him.

95 **Egeus.** Scornful Lysander, true, he hath my love;
And what is mine my love shall render him.
And she is mine, and all my right of her
I do estate unto Demetrius.

Lysander. *[to Theseus]*
I am, my lord, as well derived as he,
100 As well possessed. My love is more than his;
My fortunes every way as fairly ranked
(If not with vantage) as Demetrius';
And (which is more than all these boasts can be)
I am beloved of beauteous Hermia.
105 Why should not I then prosecute my right?

106 *avouch . . . head:* declare it to his face.

107 *Made love to:* courted.

110 *spotted and inconstant:* wicked and unfaithful.

113 *self-affairs:* my own concerns.

116 *schooling:* warning, criticism.

117 *look you arm yourself:* see that you prepare yourself.

120 *extenuate:* lessen, change.

122 *What cheer:* How are you?

125 *Against:* in preparation for.

126 *nearly that:* that closely.

129 *How chance:* how does it happen that.

130 *Belike:* perhaps; *want:* lack.

131 *Beteem:* give.

132 *For aught:* according to anything.

135 *blood:* hereditary rank.

137 *misgraffèd . . . years:* badly matched in age.

Demetrius, I'll avouch it to his head,
Made love to Nedar's daughter, Helena,
And won her soul; and she, sweet lady, dotes,
Devoutly dotes, dotes in idolatry,
110 Upon this spotted and inconstant man.

Theseus. I must confess that I have heard so much,
And with Demetrius thought to have spoke thereof;
But, being overfull of self-affairs,
My mind did lose it.—But, Demetrius, come,
115 And come, Egeus; you shall go with me.
I have some private schooling for you both.—
For you, fair Hermia, look you arm yourself
To fit your fancies to your father's will,
Or else the law of Athens yields you up
120 (Which by no means we may extenuate)
To death or to a vow of single life.—
Come, my Hippolyta. What cheer, my love?—
Demetrius and Egeus, go along.
I must employ you in some business
125 Against our nuptial, and confer with you
Of something nearly that concerns yourselves.

Egeus. With duty and desire we follow you.

[All but Hermia and Lysander exit.]

Lysander. How now, my love? Why is your cheek so
    pale?
How chance the roses there do fade so fast?

130 **Hermia.** Belike for want of rain, which I could well
Beteem them from the tempest of my eyes.

Lysander. Ay me! For aught that I could ever read,
Could ever hear by tale or history,
The course of true love never did run smooth.
135 But either it was different in blood—

Hermia. O cross! Too high to be enthralled to low.

Lysander. Or else misgraffèd in respect of years—

139 *stood upon:* depended on.

143 *momentany:* momentary.

145–149 Lysander compares ill-fated love to the effects of lightning in the blackened *(collied)* night; earth and sky are suddenly *(in a spleen)* lit up and then immediately plunge back into darkness.

150–155 Hermia says that if true lovers have always been thwarted, they should teach themselves to be patient; the thwarting is as customary as dreams, sighs, tears, and other aspects of love *(poor fancy's followers).* *How would you describe Hermia's vision of love?*

156 *persuasion:* attitude, way of looking at it.

160 *respects:* regards.

165 *without:* outside of.

167 *To do . . . May:* to celebrate May Day.

Hermia. O spite! Too old to be engaged to young.

Lysander. Or else it stood upon the choice of friends—

140　**Hermia.** O hell, to choose love by another's eyes!

Lysander. Or, if there were a sympathy in choice,
　　War, death, or sickness did lay siege to it,
　　Making it momentany as a sound,
　　Swift as a shadow, short as any dream,
145　Brief as the lightning in the collied night,
　　That, in a spleen, unfolds both heaven and earth,
　　And, ere a man hath power to say "Behold!"
　　The jaws of darkness do devour it up.
　　So quick bright things come to confusion.

150　**Hermia.** If then true lovers have been ever crossed,
　　It stands as an edict in destiny.
　　Then let us teach our trial patience
　　Because it is a customary cross,
　　As due to love as thoughts and dreams and sighs,
155　Wishes and tears, poor fancy's followers.

Lysander. A good persuasion. Therefore, hear me,
　　Hermia:
　　I have a widow aunt, a dowager
　　Of great revenue, and she hath no child.
　　From Athens is her house remote seven leagues,
160　And she respects me as her only son.
　　There, gentle Hermia, may I marry thee;
　　And to that place the sharp Athenian law
　　Cannot pursue us. If thou lovest me, then
　　Steal forth thy father's house tomorrow night,
165　And in the wood a league without the town
　　(Where I did meet thee once with Helena
　　To do observance to a morn of May),
　　There will I stay for thee.

Hermia. 　　　　　　　　My good Lysander,
　　I swear to thee by Cupid's strongest bow,
170　By his best arrow with the golden head,

169–179 In her vow to Lysander, Hermia refers to mythological figures associated with love. Cupid was said to use arrows with golden heads to make people fall in love. Venus, the goddess of love, rode in a chariot pulled by doves. Dido, the Queen of Carthage, burned herself on a pyre after being abandoned by Aeneas, a Trojan hero.

182 *your fair:* your fairness; beauty; *happy:* fortunate.

183 *lodestars:* guiding stars.

184 *tunable:* melodious.

186 Helena wishes that appearance were as contagious *(catching)* as disease.

190–191 *Were the . . . translated:* If I possessed the whole world except for Demetrius, I would give up everything to be transformed into you.

By the simplicity of Venus' doves,
By that which knitteth souls and prospers loves,
And by that fire which burned the Carthage queen
When the false Trojan under sail was seen,
175   By all the vows that ever men have broke
(In number more than ever women spoke),
In that same place thou hast appointed me,
Tomorrow truly will I meet with thee.

Lysander. Keep promise, love. Look, here comes Helena.

[Enter Helena.]

180   **Hermia.** Godspeed, fair Helena. Whither away?

Helena. Call you me "fair"? That "fair" again unsay.
Demetrius loves your fair. O happy fair!
Your eyes are lodestars and your tongue's sweet air
More tunable than lark to shepherd's ear
185   When wheat is green, when hawthorn buds appear.
Sickness is catching. O, were favor so!
Yours would I catch, fair Hermia, ere I go.
My ear should catch your voice, my eye your eye;
My tongue should catch your tongue's sweet melody.
190   Were the world mine, Demetrius being bated,
The rest I'd give to be to you translated.
O, teach me how you look and with what art
You sway the motion of Demetrius' heart!

Hermia. I frown upon him, yet he loves me still.

195   **Helena.** O, that your frowns would teach my smiles
such skill!

Hermia. I give him curses, yet he gives me love.

Helena. O, that my prayers could such affection move!

Hermia. The more I hate, the more he follows me.

Helena. The more I love, the more he hateth me.

200   **Hermia.** His folly, Helena, is no fault of mine.

201 *Would:* I wish.

206 *graces:* attractive qualities.

209–210 *Phoebe:* another name for Diana, the moon goddess, described here as staring at her reflection in a pond or lake and adorning the grass with dew.

212 *still:* always.

215 *faint:* pale; *wont:* accustomed.

216 *counsel:* secrets, private opinions.

219 *stranger companies:* the company of strangers.

223 *lovers' food:* looking at each other.

226 *o'er other some:* in comparison to some others.

Helena. None but your beauty. Would that fault were
 mine!

Hermia. Take comfort: he no more shall see my face.
 Lysander and myself will fly this place.
 Before the time I did Lysander see
205 Seemed Athens as a paradise to me.
 O, then, what graces in my love do dwell
 That he hath turned a heaven unto a hell!

Lysander. Helen, to you our minds we will unfold.
 Tomorrow night when Phoebe doth behold
210 Her silver visage in the wat'ry glass,
 Decking with liquid pearl the bladed grass
 (A time that lovers' flights doth still conceal),
 Through Athens' gates have we devised to steal.

Hermia. And in the wood where often you and I
215 Upon faint primrose beds were wont to lie,
 Emptying our bosoms of their counsel sweet,
 There my Lysander and myself shall meet,
 And thence from Athens turn away our eyes
 To seek new friends and stranger companies.
220 Farewell, sweet playfellow. Pray thou for us,
 And good luck grant thee thy Demetrius.—
 Keep word, Lysander. We must starve our sight
 From lovers' food till morrow deep midnight.

Lysander. I will, my Hermia.

[Hermia exits.]

 Helena, adieu.
225 As you on him, Demetrius dote on you!

[Lysander exits.]

Helena. How happy some o'er other some can be!
 Through Athens I am thought as fair as she.
 But what of that? Demetrius thinks not so.
 He will not know what all but he do know.
230 And, as he errs, doting on Hermia's eyes,

232 ***holding no quantity:*** out of proportion.

236–241 Helena says that Cupid is depicted as a blind boy with wings because the wings and blindness symbolize ***(figure)*** reckless haste. He is said to be a child because love is easily deceived; love also makes false vows ***(forswear)*** like those made by boys at play. *What do these comments suggest about Helena's own experience of love?*

242 ***eyne:*** eyes.

243 ***hailed down:*** poured down like hail.

248 ***intelligence:*** information.

249 ***If . . . expense:*** Helena could mean either that she will purchase his thanks at a high ***(dear)*** cost or that his thanks will be a precious ***(dear)*** purchase.

So I, admiring of his qualities.
Things base and vile, holding no quantity,
Love can transpose to form and dignity.
Love looks not with the eyes but with the mind;
235 And therefore is winged Cupid painted blind.
Nor hath Love's mind of any judgment taste.
Wings, and no eyes, figure unheedy haste.
And therefore is Love said to be a child
Because in choice he is so oft beguiled.
240 As waggish boys in game themselves forswear,
So the boy Love is perjured everywhere.
For, ere Demetrius looked on Hermia's eyne,
He hailed down oaths that he was only mine;
And when this hail some heat from Hermia felt,
245 So he dissolved, and show'rs of oaths did melt.
I will go tell him of fair Hermia's flight.
Then to the wood will he tomorrow night
Pursue her. And, for this intelligence
If I have thanks, it is a dear expense.
250 But herein mean I to enrich my pain,
To have his sight thither and back again.

[She exits.]

2 *You were best:* you ought to; ***generally:*** Bottom's error for "individually."

3 *scrip:* script.

6 *interlude:* dramatic entertainment.

10 *grow to a point:* come to a conclusion.

11 *Marry:* indeed (originally a mild oath shortened from "by the Virgin Mary").

12–13 *Pyramus and Thisbe:* This story, similar to Romeo and Juliet, is told in Ovid's *Metamorphoses*.

Scene 2 *Athens.*

A group of craftsmen headed by Peter Quince are organizing a theatrical performance for Theseus and Hippolyta's wedding festivities. The part of Pyramus will be played by Bottom the weaver, who is so confident of his acting ability that he proposes to play most of the other parts as well. After the roles are assigned, the men agree to meet in the wood the next night for a rehearsal.

[Enter Quince *the carpenter, and* Snug *the joiner, and* Bottom *the weaver, and* Flute *the bellows-mender, and* Snout *the tinker, and* Starveling *the tailor.]*

Quince. Is all our company here?

Bottom. You were best to call them generally, man by man, according to the scrip.

Quince. Here is the scroll of every man's name which
5   is thought fit, through all Athens, to play in our interlude before the Duke and the Duchess on his wedding day at night.

Bottom. First, good Peter Quince, say what the play treats on, then read the names of the actors, and so
10   grow to a point.

Quince. Marry, our play is "The most lamentable comedy and most cruel death of Pyramus and Thisbe."

Bottom. A very good piece of work, I assure you, and a merry. Now, good Peter Quince, call forth your
15   actors by the scroll. Masters, spread yourselves.

Quince. Answer as I call you. Nick Bottom, the weaver.

Bottom. Ready. Name what part I am for, and proceed.

Quince. You, Nick Bottom, are set down for Pyramus.

Bottom. What is Pyramus—a lover or a tyrant?

21 *ask:* call for.

23 *condole:* lament, grieve.

24 *humor:* inclination.

25 *Ercles:* Hercules; *tear a cat:* rant and rave.

31 *Phibbus' car:* the chariot of Phoebus Apollo, the sun god.

36 *vein:* style.

40 *take Thisbe on you:* take the part of Thisbe.

45 *That's all one:* That doesn't matter; *mask:* often worn by Elizabethan women to protect their skin from the sun.

46 *small:* high-pitched.

47 *An:* if.

48 *monstrous:* extraordinarily.

20 **Quince.** A lover that kills himself most gallant for love.

Bottom. That will ask some tears in the true performing of it. If I do it, let the audience look to their eyes. I will move storms; I will condole in some measure. To the rest.—Yet my chief humor is for a tyrant. I could
25 play Ercles rarely, or a part to tear a cat in, to make all split:

> The raging rocks
> And shivering shocks
> Shall break the locks
30 > Of prison gates.
> And Phibbus' car
> Shall shine from far
> And make and mar
> The foolish Fates.

35 This was lofty. Now name the rest of the players. This is Ercles' vein, a tyrant's vein. A lover is more condoling.

Quince. Francis Flute, the bellows-mender.

Flute. Here, Peter Quince.

40 **Quince.** Flute, you must take Thisbe on you.

Flute. What is Thisbe—a wand'ring knight?

Quince. It is the lady that Pyramus must love.

Flute. Nay, faith, let not me play a woman. I have a beard coming.

45 **Quince.** That's all one. You shall play it in a mask, and you may speak as small as you will.

Bottom. An I may hide my face, let me play Thisbe too. I'll speak in a monstrous little voice: "Thisne, Thisne!"— "Ah Pyramus, my lover dear! Thy Thisbe
50 dear and lady dear!"

Quince. No, no, you must play Pyramus—and, Flute,

61 *fitted:* a punning reference to the activities of a carpenter *(joiner).*

64 *extempore:* without notes.

76 *aggravate:* Bottom's error for "moderate."

77 *roar you:* roar for you.

77–78 *sucking dove:* Bottom confuses the sucking lamb and the sitting dove, proverbial symbols of meekness.

78 *an 'twere:* as if it were.

80 *a proper:* as handsome a.

80–83 *What impression does Quince seem to have of Bottom?*

you Thisbe.

Bottom. Well, proceed.

Quince. Robin Starveling, the tailor.

55 **Starveling.** Here, Peter Quince.

Quince. Robin Starveling, you must play Thisbe's mother.—Tom Snout, the tinker.

Snout. Here, Peter Quince.

Quince. You, Pyramus' father.—Myself, Thisbe's
60 father.—Snug the joiner, you the lion's part.—And I hope here is a play fitted.

Snug. Have you the lion's part written? Pray you, if it be, give it me, for I am slow of study.

Quince. You may do it extempore, for it is nothing but
65 roaring.

Bottom. Let me play the lion too. I will roar that I will do any man's heart good to hear me. I will roar that I will make the Duke say "Let him roar again. Let him roar again!"

70 **Quince.** An you should do it too terribly, you would fright the Duchess and the ladies that they would shriek, and that were enough to hang us all.

All. That would hang us, every mother's son.

Bottom. I grant you, friends, if you should fright the
75 ladies out of their wits, they would have no more discretion but to hang us. But I will aggravate my voice so that I will roar you as gently as any suck-ing dove. I will roar you an 'twere any nightingale.

Quince. You can play no part but Pyramus, for
80 Pyramus is a sweet-faced man, a proper man as one shall see in a summer's day, a most lovely gentlemanlike man. Therefore you must needs play Pyramus.

86 *what you will:* whatever you want.

87–90 Bottom shows off his weaver's knowledge of dyes, proposing to perform *(discharge)* the part wearing a beard that is either straw-colored, tan *(orange-tawny),* red *(purple-in-grain),* or the perfect yellow of a French gold coin *(French-crown-color).*

91–92 Quince jokingly refers to heads *(crowns)* bald from syphilis, known as the "French disease."

94 *con:* learn.

96 *without:* outside of.

98 *devices:* plans.

99–100 *bill of . . . wants:* list of stage props that our play requires.

102 *obscenely:* probably an error for "seemly," fittingly.

102–103 *Be perfit:* Be word-perfect, that is, memorize your parts completely.

105 Bottom urges them to keep their promise. (He may be using an archery term or a proverbial expression.)

Bottom. Well, I will undertake it. What beard were I
85   best to play it in?

Quince. Why, what you will.

Bottom. I will discharge it in either your straw-color
      beard, your orange-tawny beard, your purple-in-
      grain beard, or your French-crown-color beard,
90   your perfit yellow.

Quince. Some of your French crowns have no hair at
      all, and then you will play barefaced. But, masters,
      here are your parts, *[giving out the parts,]* and I am
      to entreat you, request you, and desire you, to con
95   them by tomorrow night and meet me in the palace
      wood, a mile without the town, by moonlight. There
      will we rehearse, for if we meet in the city, we shall
      be dogged with company and our devices known.
      In the meantime I will draw a bill of properties
100   such as our play wants. I pray you fail me not.

Bottom. We will meet, and there we may rehearse
      most obscenely and courageously. Take pains. Be
      perfit. Adieu.

Quince. At the Duke's Oak we meet.
105 **Bottom.** Enough. Hold, or cut bowstrings.

[They exit.]

2 *dale:* valley.

3 *Thorough:* through.

4 *pale:* fenced-in land.

7 *sphere:* orbit.

9-13 The fairy performs various services for Queen Titania, such as placing dew on fairy rings **(orbs)**—the circles of darker grass in a meadow—and putting ruby spots on the gold surfaces of cowslips, tall flowers with colors that resemble the uniform colors of the royal guard **(pensioners).** The ruby spots of the cowslips are the source of perfumes **(savors).**

16 *lob of spirits:* country bumpkin among spirits.

ACT TWO

Scene 1 *The wood near Athens.*

The king and queen of fairyland, Oberon and Titania, are quarreling over a stolen Indian boy, who is a servant to Queen Titania. Oberon orders Robin Goodfellow to fetch a special flower that makes people fall in love with the next creature they see. Oberon plans to use this love potion to trick Titania into releasing the boy. While waiting for Robin, Oberon overhears Demetrius speaking harshly to Helena. Taking pity on her, Oberon tells Robin to use some of the love potion on the Athenian youth to make him fall in love with Helena.

[Enter a Fairy *at one door and* Robin Goodfellow *at another.]*

Robin. How now, spirit? Whither wander you?

Fairy.   Over hill, over dale,
        Thorough bush, thorough brier,
     Over park, over pale,
5   Thorough flood, thorough fire;
     I do wander everywhere,
     Swifter than the moon's sphere.
     And I serve the Fairy Queen,
     To dew her orbs upon the green.
10   The cowslips tall her pensioners be;
     In their gold coats spots you see;
     Those be rubies, fairy favors;
     In those freckles live their savors.
   I must go seek some dewdrops here
15   And hang a pearl in every cowslip's ear.
   Farewell, thou lob of spirits. I'll be gone.

17 anon: soon.

18 revels: merrymaking, royal entertainment.

20 passing fell and wrath: extremely fierce and wrathful.

23 changeling: a child exchanged for another by fairies.

25 trace: travel through.

26 perforce: forcibly.

29 fountain: spring; **spangled starlight sheen:**
glittering and shining starlight.

30 square: quarrel.

34 Robin Goodfellow: a mischievous spirit or goblin,
also known as "Puck."

34–39 The Fairy lists mischievous pranks associated with
Robin, including frightening village maidens, stealing
the cream from milk, doing something to the butter
churn **(quern)** to make the housewife work in vain
(bootless), and preventing beer from forming a frothy
head **(barm).**

47–50 Robin sometimes takes the shape of a crab apple
added to hot spiced ale; when an old gossip tries to
drink from her cup **(bowl),** he bobs up and down,
making the ale spill on her neck **(dewlap).**

51 aunt: old woman.

Our queen and all her elves come here anon.

Robin. The King doth keep his revels here tonight.
Take heed the Queen come not within his sight,
20 For Oberon is passing fell and wrath
Because that she, as her attendant, hath
A lovely boy stolen from an Indian king;
She never had so sweet a changeling.
And jealous Oberon would have the child
25 Knight of his train, to trace the forests wild.
But she perforce withholds the lovèd boy,
Crowns him with flowers, and makes him all her joy.
And now they never meet in grove or green,
By fountain clear, or spangled starlight sheen,
30 But they do square, that all their elves for fear
Creep into acorn cups and hide them there.

Fairy. Either I mistake your shape and making quite,
Or else you are that shrewd and knavish sprite
Called Robin Goodfellow. Are not you he
35 That frights the maidens of the villagery,
Skim milk, and sometimes labor in the quern
And bootless make the breathless huswife churn,
And sometime make the drink to bear no barm,
Mislead night wanderers, laughing at their harm?
40 Those that "Hobgoblin" call you, and "sweet Puck,"
You do their work, and they shall have good luck.
Are not you he?

Robin.   Thou speakest aright.
I am that merry wanderer of the night.
I jest to Oberon and make him smile
45 When I a fat and bean-fed horse beguile,
Neighing in likeness of a filly foal.
And sometime lurk I in a gossip's bowl
In very likeness of a roasted crab,
And, when she drinks, against her lips I bob
50 And on her withered dewlap pour the ale.
The wisest aunt, telling the saddest tale,
Sometime for three-foot stool mistaketh me;

53 *bum:* slang for "buttocks."

54 *Tailor:* an exclamation for a sudden fall backwards.

55 *choir:* company; *loffe:* laugh.

56 *waxen:* increase; *neeze:* sneeze.

58 *room:* make room.

62 *forsworn:* renounced.

63 *Tarry:* wait there; *wanton:* headstrong creature.

66 *in the shape of Corin:* disguised as Corin (a traditional shepherd's name in love poetry).

67 *pipes of corn:* a wind instrument made from a grain stalk.

68 *Phillida:* a traditional shepherdess's name.

70–83 Titania jealously says that in truth *(forsooth),* Oberon has come from the farthest slope *(steep)* of India to bless the marriage of Hippolyta, his boot-wearing *(buskined)* mistress. Oberon accuses her of hypocrisy, saying that he knows of her love for Theseus. He names four lovers whom Theseus deserted *(Perigouna, Aegles, Ariadne, and Antiopa).* According to Oberon, Titania made Theseus break his promises *(his faith)* to these women.

81 *forgeries:* fictions.

82 *middle summer's spring:* beginning of midsummer.

Then slip I from her bum, down topples she,
And "Tailor!" cries, and falls into a cough,
55　And then the whole choir hold their hips and loffe
And waxen in their mirth and neeze and swear
A merrier hour was never wasted there.
But room, fairy. Here comes Oberon.

Fairy. And here my mistress. Would that he were
　　gone!

[*Enter* Oberon the King of Fairies *at one door, with his train, and* Titania the Queen *at another, with hers.*]

60　**Oberon.** Ill met by moonlight, proud Titania.

Titania. What, jealous Oberon? Fairies, skip hence.
I have forsworn his bed and company.

Oberon. Tarry, rash wanton. Am not I thy lord?

Titania. Then I must be thy lady. But I know
65　When thou hast stolen away from Fairyland
And in the shape of Corin sat all day
Playing on pipes of corn and versing love
To amorous Phillida. Why art thou here,
Come from the farthest steep of India,
70　But that, forsooth, the bouncing Amazon,
Your buskined mistress and your warrior love,
To Theseus must be wedded, and you come
To give their bed joy and prosperity?

Oberon. How canst thou thus for shame, Titania,
75　Glance at my credit with Hippolyta,
Knowing I know thy love to Theseus?
Didst not thou lead him through the glimmering
　　night
From Perigouna, whom he ravishèd,
And make him with fair Aegles break his faith,
80　With Ariadne and Antiopa?

Titania. These are the forgeries of jealousy;
And never, since the middle summer's spring,

83 mead: meadow.

84 pavèd fountain: a spring with a pebbled bottom.

85 margent: margin, shore.

86 ringlets: circle dances.

90 Contagious: disease-spreading.

91 pelting: paltry.

92 continents: banks.

94–95 green corn . . . beard: the grain has rotted before it could ripen.

96 fold: an enclosure for domestic animals.

97 murrain flock: a flock killed by an infectious disease.

98 nine-men's morris: a square outdoor playing area.

99–100 Because no people walk there, the intricate paths in the tall grass **(wanton green)** have become grown over.

101 want: lack.

103 Therefore: because of our quarrel.

105 rheumatic diseases: respiratory infections such as colds and flu.

106 Thorough: through; **distemperature:** disturbance in nature.

109 old Heims': winter's.

110 odorous chaplet: fragrant wreath.

112 childing: fruitful.

113 wonted liveries: usual outfits

113–114 the mazèd . . . which: The bewildered world can no longer tell the seasons apart by what they produce **(increase).**

115–116 Titania says that these evils are the offspring of their quarrel **(debate).**

117 original: origin.

Met we on hill, in dale, forest, or mead,
By pavèd fountain or by rushy brook,
85   Or in the beachèd margent of the sea,
To dance our ringlets to the whistling wind,
But with thy brawls thou hast disturbed our sport.
Therefore the winds, piping to us in vain,
As in revenge have sucked up from the sea
90   Contagious fogs, which, falling in the land,
Hath every pelting river made so proud
That they have overborne their continents.
The ox hath therefore stretched his yoke in vain,
The plowman lost his sweat, and the green corn
95   Hath rotted ere his youth attained a beard.
The fold stands empty in the drownèd field,
And crows are fatted with the murrain flock.
The nine-men's-morris is filled up with mud,
And the quaint mazes in the wanton green,
100   For lack of tread, are undistinguishable.
The human mortals want their winter here.
No night is now with hymn or carol blessed.
Therefore the moon, the governess of floods,
Pale in her anger, washes all the air,
105   That rheumatic diseases do abound.
And thorough this distemperature we see
The seasons alter: hoary-headed frosts
Fall in the fresh lap of the crimson rose,
And on old Hiems' thin and icy crown
110   An odorous chaplet of sweet summer buds
Is, as in mockery, set. The spring, the summer,
The childing autumn, angry winter, change
Their wonted liveries, and the mazèd world
By their increase now knows not which is which.
115   And this same progeny of evils comes
From our debate, from our dissension;
We are their parents and original.

Oberon. Do you amend it, then. It lies in you.
Why should Titania cross her Oberon?
120   I do but beg a little changeling boy

121 *henchman:* page, boy attendant.

122 Titania wouldn't give him up for all of Fairyland.

123 *vot'ress:* a woman pledged to a life of religious worship or service; *order:* a group dedicated to religious service.

125 *Full:* quite.

126 *Neptune:* the sea god.

127 *Marking . . . flood:* watching the merchant ships on the ocean.

129 *wanton:* lewd or immoral.

130–134 *Which she . . . merchandise:* The pregnant votress, as she walked to fetch things for Titania, resembled the ships with their full sails.

140 *round:* circle dance

142 *spare your haunts:* stay away from the places you visit.

145 *chide downright:* fight outright.

147 *injury:* insult.

149 *Since:* when; *promontory:* a rock jutting out from the sea.

To be my henchman.

Titania.   Set your heart at rest:
The Fairyland buys not the child of me.
His mother was a vot'ress of my order,
And in the spicèd Indian air by night
125 Full often hath she gossiped by my side
And sat with me on Neptune's yellow sands,
Marking th' embarkèd traders on the flood,
When we have laughed to see the sails conceive
And grow big-bellied with the wanton wind;
130 Which she, with pretty and with swimming gait,
Following (her womb then rich with my young
    squire),
Would imitate and sail upon the land
To fetch me trifles and return again,
As from a voyage, rich with merchandise.
135 But she, being mortal, of that boy did die,
And for her sake do I rear up her boy,
And for her sake I will not part with him.

Oberon. How long within this wood intend you stay?

Titania. Perchance till after Theseus' wedding day.
140 If you will patiently dance in our round
And see our moonlight revels, go with us.
If not, shun me, and I will spare your haunts.

Oberon. Give me that boy and I will go with thee.

Titania. Not for thy fairy kingdom. Fairies, away.
145 We shall chide downright if I longer stay.

[Titania and her fairies exit.]

Oberon. Well, go thy way. Thou shalt not from this
    grove
Till I torment thee for this injury.—
My gentle Puck, come hither. Thou rememb'rest
Since once I sat upon a promontory
150 And heard a mermaid on a dolphin's back

151 *dulcet:* pleasant; *breath:* voice.

153 *spheres:* orbits.

157-165 Oberon tells of the time he saw Cupid shoot a fiery love arrow *(love-shaft)* at a virgin *(vestal),* probably an allusion to Elizabeth I, the Virgin Queen. However, the fire was extinguished by the beams of the moon (associated with the virgin goddess of Diana), and Cupid's arrow missed its mark, leaving the virgin free of love's power *(fancy-free). What does this passage suggest about the power of love?*

165 *bolt:* arrow.

168 *love-in-idleness:* the pansy.

171 *or . . . or:* either . . . or.

174 *leviathan:* sea monster, whale; *league:* approximately three miles.

175 *I'll put . . . earth:* I'll circle the earth.

Uttering such dulcet and harmonious breath
That the rude sea grew civil at her song
And certain stars shot madly from their spheres
To hear the sea-maid's music.

Robin.   I remember.

155 **Oberon.** That very time I saw (but thou couldst not),
Flying between the cold moon and the earth,
Cupid all armed. A certain aim he took
At a fair vestal thronèd by the west,
And loosed his love-shaft smartly from his bow
160 As it should pierce a hundred thousand hearts.
But I might see young Cupid's fiery shaft
Quenched in the chaste beams of the wat'ry moon,
And the imperial vot'ress passèd on
In maiden meditation, fancy-free.
165 Yet marked I where the bolt of Cupid fell.
It fell upon a little western flower,
Before, milk-white, now purple with love's wound,
And maidens call it "love-in-idleness."
Fetch me that flower; the herb I showed thee once.
170 The juice of it on sleeping eyelids laid
Will make or man or woman madly dote
Upon the next live creature that it sees.
Fetch me this herb, and be thou here again
Ere the leviathan can swim a league.

175 **Robin.** I'll put a girdle round about the earth
In forty minutes.

[He exits.]

Oberon.   Having once this juice,
I'll watch Titania when she is asleep
And drop the liquor of it in her eyes.
The next thing then she, waking, looks upon
180 (Be it on lion, bear, or wolf, or bull,
On meddling monkey, or on busy ape)
She shall pursue it with the soul of love.
And ere I take this charm from off her sight

185 *page:* boy attendant.

190 Demetrius hopes to stop *(stay)* Lysander before he has
a chance to marry Hermia, whose attractive power
holds *(stayeth)* Demetrius.

192 *and wood:* and mad.

195 *adamant:* magnet.

197 *Leave you:* give up.

199 *speak you fair:* speak courteously to you.

201 *nor:* and.

214 *impeach:* call into question.

(As I can take it with another herb),
185 I'll make her render up her page to me.
But who comes here? I am invisible,
And I will overhear their conference.

[Enter Demetrius, Helena *following him.*]

Demetrius. I love thee not; therefore pursue me not.
Where is Lysander and fair Hermia?
190 The one I'll stay; the other stayeth me.
Thou told'st me they were stol'n unto this wood,
And here am I, and wood within this wood
Because I cannot meet my Hermia.
Hence, get thee gone, and follow me no more.

195 **Helena.** You draw me, you hard-hearted adamant!
But yet you draw not iron, for my heart
Is true as steel. Leave you your power to draw,
And I shall have no power to follow you.

Demetrius. Do I entice you? Do I speak you fair?
200 Or rather do I not in plainest truth
Tell you I do not, nor I cannot love you?

Helena. And even for that do I love you the more.
I am your spaniel, and, Demetrius,
The more you beat me I will fawn on you.
205 Use me but as your spaniel: spurn me, strike me,
Neglect me, lose me; only give me leave
(Unworthy as I am) to follow you.
What worser place can I beg in your love
(And yet a place of high respect with me)
210 Than to be usèd as you use your dog?

Demetrius. Tempt not too much the hatred of my spirit,
For I am sick when I do look on thee.

Helena. And I am sick when I look not on you.

Demetrius. You do impeach your modesty too much
215 To leave the city and commit yourself
Into the hands of one that loves you not,

218 *desert:* deserted, uninhabited.

220–226 Helena says that his excellence gives her the right to be in the wood at night. When she looks at his face, she feels as if it is no longer night; she does not feel alone here, since from her perspective he is the whole world. *How would you characterize Helena's judgment so far?*

227 *brakes:* thickets.

231 In classical mythology, Daphne was chased by the god Apollo; after praying for help, she was transformed into a laurel tree. In this and her other two examples, Helena changes the stories to show the weak pursuing the strong.

232 *griffin:* a mythical monster with the head and wings of an eagle and the body of a lion; *hind:* female deer.

233 *Bootless:* useless.

235 *stay thy questions:* wait to hear your argument.

236–237 *do not . . . But:* be assured that; *mischief:* harm.

240 *Your wrongs . . . sex:* Your wrongdoing has led me to act in a way that disgraces all women.

244 *upon:* by.

To trust the opportunity of night
And the ill counsel of a desert place
With the rich worth of your virginity.

220 **Helena.** Your virtue is my privilege. For that
It is not night when I do see your face
Therefore I think I am not in the night.
Nor doth this wood lack worlds of company,
For you, in my respect, are all the world.
225 Then, how can it be said I am alone
When all the world is here to look on me?

Demetrius. I'll run from thee and hide me in the brakes
And leave thee to the mercy of wild beasts.

Helena. The wildest hath not such a heart as you.
230 Run when you will. The story shall be changed:
Apollo flies and Daphne holds the chase;
The dove pursues the griffin; the mild hind
Makes speed to catch the tiger. Bootless speed
When cowardice pursues and valor flies!

235 **Demetrius.** I will not stay thy questions. Let me go,
Or if thou follow me, do not believe
But I shall do thee mischief in the wood.

Helena. Ay, in the temple, in the town, the field,
You do me mischief. Fie, Demetrius!
240 Your wrongs do set a scandal on my sex.
We cannot fight for love as men may do.
We should be wooed and were not made to woo.

[Demetrius exits.]

I'll follow thee and make a heaven of hell
To die upon the hand I love so well.

[Helena exits.]

245 **Oberon.** Fare thee well, nymph. Ere he do leave this
grove,
Thou shalt fly him, and he shall seek thy love.

251 *oxlips:* flowers that resemble the cowslip.

252 *woodbine:* honeysuckle.

253 *muskroses:* large, fragrant roses; *eglantine:* sweetbrier (a kind of rose).

254 *sometime of:* sometimes during.

256 *throws:* casts, sheds; *her:* its.

257 *Weed:* garment.

258 *this:* the flower; *streak:* smear, anoint.

263 *espies:* catches sight of.

267 *fond on:* desperately in love with.

[Enter Robin.]

Hast thou the flower there? Welcome, wanderer.

Robin. Ay, there it is.

Oberon. I pray thee give it me.

[Robin gives him the flower.]

250   I know a bank where the wild thyme blows,
Where oxlips and the nodding violet grows,
Quite overcanopied with luscious woodbine,
With sweet muskroses, and with eglantine.
There sleeps Titania sometime of the night,
255   Lulled in these flowers with dances and delight.
And there the snake throws her enameled skin,
Weed wide enough to wrap a fairy in.
And with the juice of this I'll streak her eyes
And make her full of hateful fantasies.
260   Take thou some of it, and seek through this grove.

[He gives Robin part of the flower.]

A sweet Athenian lady is in love
With a disdainful youth. Anoint his eyes,
But do it when the next thing he espies
May be the lady. Thou shalt know the man
265   By the Athenian garments he hath on.
Effect it with some care, that he may prove
More fond on her than she upon her love.
And look thou meet me ere the first cock crow.

Robin. Fear not, my lord. Your servant shall do so.

[They exit.]

1–8 Titania announces that after a circle dance **(roundel)** and a song, she will rest for 20 seconds while her fairies go off to do various duties **(offices).**

3 ***cankers:*** cankerworms.

4 ***reremice:*** bats.

7 ***quaint:*** dainty.

9 ***double:*** forked.

11 ***Newts*** (a type of salamander) and ***blindworms*** (small snakes) are harmless, but in Shakespeare's day they were considered poisonous.

13 ***Philomel:*** the nightingale. (In classical mythology, Philomela was transformed into a nightingale.)

Scene 2 *The wood.*

After Titania falls asleep, Oberon anoints her eyes with the flower's nectar. Meanwhile Lysander and Hermia stop to sleep nearby. Robin comes along and anoints Lysander's eyes, assuming that he is the Athenian youth described by Oberon. Robin has just missed seeing his real target, Demetrius, who finally manages to leave Helena behind as he passes through. When Helena notices Lysander on the ground, she wakes him and he immediately falls in love with her. She mistakes his affection for mockery and walks away, to be pursued by Lysander. Then the deserted Hermia wakes up from a nightmare. Finding herself all alone, she goes off in search of Lysander.

[Enter Titania, Queen of Fairies, *with her train.]*

Titania. Come, now a roundel and a fairy song;
　　Then, for the third part of a minute, hence—
　　Some to kill cankers in the muskrose buds,
　　Some war with reremice for their leathern wings
5　　To make my small elves coats, and some keep back
　　The clamorous owl that nightly hoots and wonders
　　At our quaint spirits. Sing me now asleep.
　　Then to your offices and let me rest.

[She lies down.]

[Fairies sing.]

First Fairy.
　　You spotted snakes with double tongue,
10　　　*Thorny hedgehogs, be not seen.*
　　Newts and blindworms, do no wrong,
　　　Come not near our Fairy Queen.

Chorus.
　　　Philomel, with melody
　　　Sing in our sweet lullaby.
15　*Lulla, lulla, lullaby, lulla, lulla, lullaby.*
　　　Never harm

23 *offence:* harm.

28–29 *Nor spell . . . nigh:* Neither spell nor charm come near our lovely lady.

32 *aloof:* at a distance, withdrawn.

36 *ounce:* lynx.

37 *Pard:* leopard.

38 *that:* that which.

> *Nor spell nor charm*
> *Come our lovely lady nigh.*
> *So good night, with lullaby.*

First Fairy.
20 *Weaving spiders, come not here.*
> *Hence, you long-legged spinners, hence.*
> *Beetles black, approach not near.*
> *Worm nor snail, do no offence.*

Chorus.
> *Philomel, with melody*
25 *Sing in our sweet lullaby.*
> *Lulla, lulla, lullaby, lulla, lulla, lullaby.*
> *Never harm*
> *Nor spell nor charm*
> *Come our lovely lady nigh.*
30 *So good night, with lullaby.*

[Titania sleeps.]

Second Fairy. Hence, away! Now all is well.
> One aloof stand sentinel.

[Fairies exit.]

[Enter Oberon, who anoints Titania's eyelids with the nectar.]

Oberon. What thou seest when thou dost wake,
> Do it for thy true love take.
35 Love and languish for his sake.
> Be it ounce, or cat, or bear,
> Pard, or boar with bristled hair,
> In thy eye that shall appear
> When thou wak'st, it is thy dear.
40 Wake when some vile thing is near.

[He exits.]

[Enter Lysander and Hermia.]

Lysander. Fair love, you faint with wand'ring in the

42 *troth:* pledge of faithfulness.

51 *take . . . innocence:* understand that my intentions are innocent.

52 *Love . . . conference:* In a conversation between lovers, everything needs to be understood in terms of their love.

58 *lying:* reclining; *lie:* tell a lie, deceive.

60 *beshrew:* curse (in a mild sense).

61–67 *Why does Hermia insist that they sleep apart?*

63 *human:* courteous.

70 Lysander lies down some distance apart from her.

71 *With half . . . pressed:* Let us share that wish, so that your eyes are also closed *(pressed).*

wood.
And, to speak troth, I have forgot our way.
We'll rest us, Hermia, if you think it good,
And tarry for the comfort of the day.

45 **Hermia.** Be it so, Lysander. Find you out a bed,
For I upon this bank will rest my head.

Lysander. One turf shall serve as pillow for us both;
One heart, one bed, two bosoms, and one troth.

Hermia. Nay, good Lysander. For my sake, my dear,
50 Lie further off yet. Do not lie so near.

Lysander. O, take the sense, sweet, of my innocence!
Love takes the meaning in love's conference.
I mean that my heart unto yours is knit,
So that but one heart we can make of it;
55 Two bosoms interchainèd with an oath—
So then two bosoms and a single troth.
Then by your side no bed-room me deny,
For lying so, Hermia, I do not lie.

Hermia. Lysander riddles very prettily.
60 Now much beshrew my manners and my pride
If Hermia meant to say Lysander lied.
But, gentle friend, for love and courtesy,
Lie further off in human modesty.
Such separation, as may well be said,
65 Becomes a virtuous bachelor and a maid.
So far be distant; and good night, sweet friend.
Thy love ne'er alter till thy sweet life end!

Lysander. "Amen, amen" to that fair prayer, say I,
And then end life when I end loyalty!
70 Here is my bed. Sleep give thee all his rest!

Hermia. With half that wish the wisher's eyes be pressed!

[They sleep.]

[Enter Robin.]

74 *approve:* test.

77 *Weeds:* garments.

84 *Churl:* ill-mannered fellow.
85 *owe:* own, possess.

86–87 *let love . . . eyelid:* May love so obsess you that it banishes sleep from your eyes.

91 *charge:* command; *haunt:* hang about.

92 *darkling:* in the dark.

94 *fond:* foolish, doting.
95 *the lesser is my grace:* the less favor I obtain.

97 *attractive:* magnetic.

Robin. Through the forest have I gone,
    But Athenian found I none
    On whose eyes I might approve
75   This flower's force in stirring love.

[He sees Lysander.*]*

    Night and silence! Who is here?
    Weeds of Athens he doth wear.
    This is he my master said
    Despisèd the Athenian maid.
80   And here the maiden, sleeping sound
    On the dank and dirty ground.
    Pretty soul, she durst not lie
    Near this lack-love, this kill-courtesy.—
    Churl, upon thy eyes I throw
85   All the power this charm doth owe.

[He anoints Lysander's *eyelids with the nectar.]*

    When thou wak'st, let love forbid
    Sleep his seat on thy eyelid.
    So, awake when I am gone,
    For I must now to Oberon.

[He exits.]

[Enter Demetrius *and* Helena, *running.]*

90 **Helena.** Stay, though thou kill me, sweet Demetrius.

Demetrius. I charge thee, hence, and do not haunt me
    thus.

Helena. O, wilt thou darkling leave me? Do not so.

Demetrius. Stay, on thy peril. I alone will go.

[Demetrius exits.]

Helena. O, I am out of breath in this fond chase.
95   The more my prayer, the lesser is my grace.
    Happy is Hermia, wheresoe'er she lies,
    For she hath blessèd and attractive eyes.

102–103 *no marvel . . . thus:* No wonder that Demetrius flees from me as if I were monster. *Why do you think Helena judges herself so harshly?*

104 *glass:* mirror.

105 *compare:* try to compete with; *sphery eyne:* starry eyes.

110–111 Lysander declares that nature performs magic *(art)* by making Helena transparent so that he can see her heart.

120 *change:* exchange.

121 *will:* desire.

123–128 Lysander says that just as growing things are not ripe until their season, before now he had not ripened to reason, but now he has reached the height *(point)* of human judgment *(skill),* and reason escorts his desire to its proper place.

129 *Wherefore:* why.

129–140 *Why does Helena assume that he is mocking her?*

How came her eyes so bright? Not with salt tears.
If so, my eyes are oftener washed than hers.
100 No, no, I am as ugly as a bear,
For beasts that meet me run away for fear.
Therefore no marvel though Demetrius
Do as a monster fly my presence thus.
What wicked and dissembling glass of mine
105 Made me compare with Hermia's sphery eyne?
But who is here? Lysander, on the ground!
Dead or asleep? I see no blood, no wound.—
Lysander, if you live, good sir, awake.

Lysander [*waking up*]. And run through fire I will for
thy sweet sake.
110 Transparent Helena! Nature shows art,
That through thy bosom makes me see thy heart.
Where is Demetrius? O, how fit a word
Is that vile name to perish on my sword!

Helena. Do not say so. Lysander, say not so.
115 What though he love your Hermia? Lord, what
though?
Yet Hermia still loves you. Then be content.

Lysander. Content with Hermia? No, I do repent
The tedious minutes I with her have spent.
Not Hermia, but Helena I love.
120 Who will not change a raven for a dove?
The will of man is by his reason swayed,
And reason says you are the worthier maid.
Things growing are not ripe until their season;
So I, being young, till now ripe not to reason.
125 And touching now the point of human skill,
Reason becomes the marshal to my will
And leads me to your eyes, where I o'erlook
Love's stories written in love's richest book.

Helena. Wherefore was I to this keen mockery born?
130 When at your hands did I deserve this scorn?
Is't not enough, is't not enough, young man,

135 *Good troth, good sooth:* indeed, really.

137 *Perforce:* of necessity.

138 *I thought . . . gentleness:* I thought you had greater courtesy.

143 *surfeit:* excess.

145–146 *the heresies . . . deceive:* Renounced heresies are hated most by those who had mistakenly believed in them.

148 *Of:* by.

149 *address:* apply.

156 *prey:* attack.

159 *an if:* if.

160 *of all loves:* for all love's sake.

161 *nigh:* near.

That I did never, no, nor never can
Deserve a sweet look from Demetrius' eye,
But you must flout my insufficiency?
135 Good troth, you do me wrong, good sooth, you do,
In such disdainful manner me to woo.
But fare you well. Perforce I must confess
I thought you lord of more true gentleness.
O, that a lady of one man refused
140 Should of another therefore be abused!

[She exits.]

Lysander. She sees not Hermia.—Hermia, sleep thou
 there,
And never mayst thou come Lysander near.
For, as a surfeit of the sweetest things
The deepest loathing to the stomach brings,
145 Or as the heresies that men do leave
Are hated most of those they did deceive,
So thou, my surfeit and my heresy,
Of all be hated, but the most of me!
And, all my powers, address your love and might
150 To honor Helen and to be her knight.

[He exits.]

Hermia *[waking up].* Help me, Lysander, help me! Do
 thy best
To pluck this crawling serpent from my breast.
Ay me, for pity! What a dream was here!
Lysander, look how I do quake with fear.
155 Methought a serpent ate my heart away,
And you sat smiling at his cruel prey.
Lysander! What, removed? Lysander, lord!
What, out of hearing? Gone? No sound, no word?
Alack, where are you? Speak, an if you hear.
160 Speak, of all loves! I swoon almost with fear.—
No? Then I well perceive you are not nigh.
Either death or you I'll find immediately.

[She exits.]

Clowns: *actors who played comical rustic characters*

2 **Pat:** on the dot, punctually; **marvels:** marvelously.

3 **plot:** piece of ground.

4 **brake:** thicket; **tiring-house:** backstage dressing area.

7 **bully:** worthy.

12 **By 'r lakin:** by our lady (an oath); **parlous:** perilous, terrible.

14 **when all is done:** when all is said and done.

ACT THREE

Scene 1 *The wood.*

Bottom and the other craftsmen hold a rehearsal in the woods. Robin overhears their clumsy performance and decides to have some fun. He transforms Bottom's head into that of an ass. When the others see him, they run off and Robin chases after them. Bottom sings to show that he isn't afraid. Awakened by his song, Titania sees Bottom and falls in love. She lures him to her bower with promises of luxury.

[With Titania *still asleep onstage, enter the* Clowns, Bottom, Quince, Snout, Starveling, Snug, *and* Flute.*]*

Bottom. Are we all met?

Quince. Pat, pat. And here's a marvels convenient place for our rehearsal. This green plot shall be our stage, this hawthorn brake our tiring-house, and we will
5   do it in action as we will do it before the Duke.

Bottom. Peter Quince?

Quince. What sayest thou, bully Bottom?

Bottom. There are things in this comedy of Pyramus and Thisbe that will never please. First, Pyramus
10   must draw a sword to kill himself, which the ladies cannot abide. How answer you that?

Snout. By 'r lakin, a parlous fear.

Starveling. I believe we must leave the killing out, when all is done.

15 **Bottom.** Not a whit! I have a device to make all well. Write me a prologue, and let the prologue seem to

23 *eight and six:* alternating lines of eight and six syllables (the standard ballad measure).

38 *defect:* Bottom's error for "effect."

40–41 *My life for yours:* I pledge my life upon your safety.

41–42 *it were . . . life:* it would be a pity that I should live.

say we will do no harm with our swords, and that
Pyramus is not killed indeed. And, for the more
better assurance, tell them that I, Pyramus, am not
20   Pyramus, but Bottom the weaver. This will put
them out of fear.

Quince. Well, we will have such a prologue, and it
shall be written in eight and six.

Bottom. No, make it two more. Let it be written in
25   eight and eight.

Snout. Will not the ladies be afeard of the lion?

Starveling. I fear it, I promise you.

Bottom. Masters, you ought to consider with yourself,
to bring in (God shield us!) a lion among ladies is a
30   most dreadful thing. For there is not a more fearful
wildfowl than your lion living, and we ought to
look to 't.

Snout. Therefore another prologue must tell he is not
a lion.

35   **Bottom.** Nay, you must name his name, and half his
face must be seen through the lion's neck, and he
himself must speak through, saying thus, or to the
same defect: "Ladies," or "Fair ladies, I would
wish you," or "I would request you," or "I would
40   entreat you not to fear, not to tremble! My life for
yours. If you think I come hither as a lion, it were
pity of my life. No, I am no such thing. I am a man
as other men are." And there indeed let him name
his name and tell them plainly he is Snug the joiner.

45   **Quince.** Well, it shall be so. But there is two hard
things: that is, to bring the moonlight into a chamber, for you know Pyramus and Thisbe meet by
moonlight.

Snout. Doth the moon shine that night we play our play?

57–58 The "man on the moon" was often depicted as a man carrying a bundle of sticks and a lantern, accompanied by his dog.

57 *disfigure:* Quince's error for "figure."

58 *present:* represent.

65–66 *loam, roughcast:* compounds used for plastering walls.

74 *hempen homespuns:* rustics dressed in homespun cloth made from hemp.

75 *cradle:* the bower where Titania is sleeping.

76 *toward:* about to begin, in preparation; *auditor:* listener.

50 **Bottom.** A calendar, a calendar! Look in the almanac. Find out moonshine, find out moonshine.

[Quince takes out a book.]

Quince. Yes, it doth shine that night.

Bottom. Why, then, may you leave a casement of the great chamber window, where we play, open, and
55 the moon may shine in at the casement.

Quince. Ay, or else one must come in with a bush of thorns and a lantern and say he comes to disfigure or to present the person of Moonshine. Then there is another thing: we must have a wall in the great
60 chamber, for Pyramus and Thisbe, says the story, did talk through the chink of a wall.

Snout. You can never bring in a wall. What say you, Bottom?

Bottom. Some man or other must present Wall. And
65 let him have some plaster, or some loam, or some roughcast about him to signify wall, or let him hold his fingers thus, and through that cranny shall Pyramus and Thisbe whisper.

Quince. If that may be, then all is well. Come, sit
70 down, every mother's son, and rehearse your parts. Pyramus, you begin. When you have spoken your speech, enter into that brake, and so everyone according to his cue.

[Enter Robin invisible to those onstage.]

Robin *[aside].* What hempen homespuns have we
     swagg'ring here
75 So near the cradle of the Fairy Queen?
What, a play toward? I'll be an auditor—
An actor too perhaps, if I see cause.

Quince. Speak, Pyramus.—Thisbe, stand forth.

Bottom *[as Pyramus]. Thisbe, the flowers of odious*

84 *by and by:* soon.

87 *marry:* indeed.

91 *triumphant brier:* magnificent wild rose bush.

92 *brisky juvenal:* lively youth; *eke:* also; *Jew:* probably an absurd attempt to rhyme with *hue* (line 92).

94–95 *Ninus:* Quince points out Flute's error of calling the legendary founder of the ancient city of Nineveh *Ninny,* which means "fool." According to Ovid's version of the story, Pyramus and Thisbe meet at the tomb of Ninus.

96–98 Each actor was given a script that contained only his speeches and their cues (a few words from the line preceding a speech to signal the actor when to begin).

99 *with the ass-head:* wearing the head of an ass.

100 *were only:* would only be.

savors sweet—

80 **Quince.** Odors, odors!

Bottom *[as* Pyramus*]. . . . odors savors sweet.
So hath thy breath, my dearest Thisbe dear.—
But hark, a voice! Stay thou but here awhile,
And by and by I will to thee appear.*

[He exits.]

85 **Robin** *[aside].* A stranger Pyramus than e'er played here.

[He exits.]

Flute. Must I speak now?

Quince. Ay, marry, must you, for you must understand
he goes but to see a noise that he heard and is to
come again.

90 **Flute** *[as* Thisbe*]. Most radiant Pyramus, most lily-
white of hue,
Of color like the red rose on triumphant brier,
Most brisky juvenal and eke most lovely Jew,
As true as truest horse, that yet would never tire.
I'll meet thee, Pyramus, at Ninny's tomb.*

95 **Quince.** "Ninus' tomb," man! Why, you must not
speak that yet. That you answer to Pyramus. You
speak all your part at once, cues and all.—Pyramus,
enter. Your cue is past. It is "never tire."

Flute. O! *[As* Thisbe*.] As true as truest horse, that yet
would never tire.*

[Enter Robin, *and* Bottom *as* Pyramus *with the ass-head.]*

100 **Bottom** *[as* Pyramus*]. If I were fair, fair Thisbe, I were
only thine.*

Quince. O monstrous! O strange! We are haunted.
Pray, masters, fly, masters! Help!

103 *about a round:* in a circle.

104 *brake:* thicket.

112 *translated:* transformed.

118 *ouzel cock:* male blackbird.

120 *throstle:* thrush.

121 *quill:* piping song (literally, a reed pipe).

[Quince, Flute, Snout, Snug, and Starveling *exit.]*

Robin. I'll follow you. I'll lead you about a round,
    Through bog, through bush, through brake,
    through brier.
105 Sometime a horse I'll be, sometime a hound,
    A hog, a headless bear, sometime a fire,
    And neigh, and bark, and grunt, and roar, and burn,
    Like horse, hound, hog, bear, fire, at every turn.

[He exits.]

Bottom. Why do they run away? This is a knavery of
    them to make me afeard.

[Enter Snout.]

110 **Snout.** O Bottom, thou art changed! What do I see on
    thee?

Bottom. What do you see? You see an ass-head of
    your own, do you?

[Snout exits.]

[Enter Quince.]

Quince. Bless thee, Bottom, bless thee! Thou art trans-
    lated!

[He exits.]

Bottom. I see their knavery. This is to make an ass of
    me, to fright me, if they could. But I will not stir
115 from this place, do what they can. I will walk up
    and down here, and I will sing, that they shall hear
    I am not afraid.
    [He sings.] The ouzel cock, so black of hue,
        With orange-tawny bill,
120   *The throstle with his note so true,*
        The wren with little quill—

Titania *[waking up].* What angel wakes me from my
    flow'ry bed?

124 *plainsong cuckoo gray:* the gray cuckoo with its simple song.

125–126 *Whose note . . . "nay":* whose song many men have noticed and dared not deny. (Supposedly, the cuckoo's cry tells a man that he is a cuckold—married to an unfaithful wife.)

127 *set his wit to:* use his intelligence to answer (echoing the proverbial warning not to set one's wits against a fool's).

128 *give a bird the lie:* accuse a bird of lying.

129 *never so:* ever so often.

133 *thy fair . . . move me:* the power of your attractiveness forces me.

137 *keep . . . together:* seldom associate with each other.

139 *gleek:* make a joke.

141–143 *How does Bottom seem to feel about the situation he finds himself in?*

143 *turn:* need, purpose.

146 *rate:* rank, value.

147 Titania says that the summer always waits upon her (that is, the seasons do her bidding).

152–153 She promises to turn him into a spirit by purifying his physical nature *(mortal grossness).*

154 Each fairy is named after something tiny or hard to see: *Peaseblossom:* the flower of the pea plant; *Mote:* speck.

Bottom [sings]. The finch, the sparrow, and the lark,
         The plainsong cuckoo gray,
125   Whose note full many a man doth mark
         And dares not answer "nay"—
for, indeed, who would set his wit to so foolish a bird?
Who would give a bird the lie though he cry "cuckoo"
never so?

130 **Titania.** I pray thee, gentle mortal, sing again.
Mine ear is much enamored of thy note,
So is mine eye enthrallèd to thy shape,
And thy fair virtue's force perforce doth move me
On the first view to say, to swear, I love thee.

135 **Bottom.** Methinks, mistress, you should have little reason
for that. And yet, to say the truth, reason and love
keep little company together nowadays. The more the
pity that some honest neighbors will not make them
friends. Nay, I can gleek upon occasion.

140 **Titania.** Thou art as wise as thou art beautiful.

Bottom. Not so neither; but if I had wit enough to get
out of this wood, I have enough to serve mine
own turn.

Titania. Out of this wood do not desire to go.
145 Thou shalt remain here whether thou wilt or no.
I am a spirit of no common rate.
The summer still doth tend upon my state,
And I do love thee. Therefore go with me.
I'll give thee fairies to attend on thee,
150 And they shall fetch thee jewels from the deep
And sing while thou on pressèd flowers dost sleep.
And I will purge thy mortal grossness so
That thou shalt like an airy spirit go.—
Peaseblossom, Cobweb, Mote, and Mustardseed!

[Enter four Fairies: Peaseblossom, Cobweb, Mote, and
Mustardseed.]

155 **Peaseblossom.** Ready.

161 Titania tells them to hop in his path and skip about before him.

162 *apricocks:* apricots; *dewberries:* blackberries.

164 *humble-bees:* bumblebees.

165–167 When Bottom goes to bed and wakes, Titania wants him to have candles made from the waxy thighs of bees and lit from the glow of fireflies.

175 *I cry . . . mercy:* I beg your pardon.

177 *I shall . . . acquaintance:* I shall want to be better acquainted with you.

178–179 *If I . . . you:* Cobwebs were used as a home remedy to stop bleeding.

181 *Squash:* an unripe pea pod.

182 *Peascod:* a ripe pea pod.

Cobweb. And I.

Mote. And I.

Mustardseed. And I.

All. Where shall we go?

160 **Titania.** Be kind and courteous to this gentleman.
　　　　Hop in his walks and gambol in his eyes;
　　　　Feed him with apricocks and dewberries,
　　　　With purple grapes, green figs, and mulberries;
　　　　The honey-bags steal from the humble-bees,
165 　　And for night-tapers crop their waxen thighs
　　　　And light them at the fiery glowworms' eyes
　　　　To have my love to bed and to arise;
　　　　And pluck the wings from painted butterflies
　　　　To fan the moonbeams from his sleeping eyes.
170 　　Nod to him, elves, and do him courtesies.

Peaseblossom. Hail, mortal!

Cobweb. Hail!

Mote. Hail!

Mustardseed. Hail!

175 **Bottom.** I cry your Worships mercy, heartily.—I
　　　　beseech your Worship's name.

Cobweb. Cobweb.

Bottom. I shall desire you of more acquaintance, good
　　　　Master Cobweb. If I cut my finger, I shall make
　　　　bold with you.—Your name, honest gentleman?

180 **Peaseblossom.** Peaseblossom.

Bottom. I pray you, commend me to Mistress Squash,
　　　　your mother, and to Master Peascod, your father.
　　　　Good Master Peaseblossom, I shall desire you of
　　　　more acquaintance, too.—Your name, I beseech
185 　　you, sir?

188–190 Bottom refers to the use of mustard (made from mustard seed) to flavor beef.

194–196 Titania says that the moon seems to be weeping over some violated *(enforcèd)* chastity, and when the moon weeps, all the flowers weep in sympathy. (Perhaps she asks for Bottom to be kept silent out of respect for the chaste moon.)

Mustardseed. Mustardseed.

Bottom. Good Master Mustardseed, I know your
patience well. That same cowardly, giantlike ox-
beef hath devoured many a gentleman of your
190   house. I promise you, your kindred hath made my
eyes water ere now. I desire you of more acquaintance, good Master Mustardseed.

Titania. Come, wait upon him. Lead him to my bower.
The moon, methinks, looks with a wat'ry eye,
195   And when she weeps, weeps every little flower,
Lamenting some enforcèd chastity.
Tie up my lover's tongue. Bring him silently.

[They exit.]

Scene 2 *The wood.*

*Although Oberon is pleased to learn of Titania's
infatuation with Bottom, he soon realizes that Robin
mistakenly applied the magic nectar to the wrong
Athenian. He sends Robin to bring Helena while he
anoints the eyes of Demetrius, who has fallen asleep after
quarreling with Hermia. Helena enters with Lysander. As
Lysander woos her, Demetrius wakes up and falls in love
with Helena. Each man claims that he is Helena's only
true lover. They are interrupted by the arrival of Hermia,
who is shocked to hear that Lysander hates her now.
Helena believes she is being mocked by all three of them.
After Lysander challenges Demetrius to a duel, Hermia
threatens to harm Helena for stealing her lover. The men
go off to fight, and Helena flees, pursued by Hermia.
Oberon orders Robin to lead them separately astray
through a dense fog until they are worn out. After the
Athenians have fallen asleep, Robin anoints Lysander's
eyes with an herb that removes the effects of the love
potion.*

3 *in extremity:* to the greatest degree.

5 *night-rule:* affairs of the night; *haunted:* much visited.

7 *close:* secluded, hidden; *consecrated:* sacred.

8 *dull:* drowsy.

9–10 Robin describes the actors as a crew of fools *(patches),* uneducated laborers *(rude mechanicals)* who earn their money in the Athenian market booths.

13 *barren sort:* stupid crew.

14 *sport:* entertainment.

15–17 *Forsook . . . head:* Robin took advantage of Bottom's exit from the playing area to put an ass's head *(noll)* on his head.

18 *Anon:* soon.

19 *mimic:* burlesque actor.

19–24 Robin compares the startled actors to geese that spot a bird hunter sneaking up on them and to a large flock of crows with reddish-brown heads *(russet-pated choughs)* scattering into the sky at the sound of a gun going off.

25 *our stamp:* the stamping of my foot.

27–28 *Their sense . . . wrong:* Due to their weak understanding and strong fears, they began to think that inanimate objects were harming them.

30 *from yielders . . . catch:* Everything preys upon cowards.

32 *translated:* transformed.

[Enter Oberon, King of Fairies.]

Oberon. I wonder if Titania be awaked;
    Then what it was that next came in her eye,
    Which she must dote on in extremity.

[Enter Robin Goodfellow.]

    Here comes my messenger. How now, mad spirit?
5   What night-rule now about this haunted grove?

Robin. My mistress with a monster is in love.
    Near to her close and consecrated bower,
    While she was in her dull and sleeping hour,
    A crew of patches, rude mechanicals,
10   That work for bread upon Athenian stalls,
    Were met together to rehearse a play
    Intended for great Theseus' nuptial day.
    The shallowest thick-skin of that barren sort,
    Who Pyramus presented in their sport,
15   Forsook his scene and entered in a brake.
    When I did him at this advantage take,
    An ass's noll I fixèd on his head.
    Anon his Thisbe must be answerèd,
    And forth my mimic comes. When they him spy,
20   As wild geese that the creeping fowler eye,
    Or russet-pated choughs, many in sort,
    Rising and cawing at the gun's report,
    Sever themselves and madly sweep the sky,
    So at his sight away his fellows fly,
25   And, at our stamp, here o'er and o'er one falls.
    He "Murder" cries and help from Athens calls.
    Their sense thus weak, lost with their fears thus
        strong,
    Made senseless things begin to do them wrong;
    For briers and thorns at their apparel snatch,
30   Some sleeves, some hats, from yielders all things
        catch.
    I led them on in this distracted fear
    And left sweet Pyramus translated there.

35 *falls out:* happens.

36 *latched:* snared, captured.

40 *That:* so that; *of force:* by necessity.

41 *close:* hidden.

48–49 *Being . . . too:* Since you have already waded into blood up to your ankles, plunge in further by killing me too.

52–55 Hermia would as soon believe that Lysander abandoned her as she would believe that the moon could creep through a hole bored into the earth and disrupt the noontime sun *(Her brother's noontide)* for the people at the opposite side of the earth *(th' Antipodes).*

57 *dead:* deadly, deathly pale.

62 *What's this to:* what does this have to do with.

When in that moment, so it came to pass,
Titania waked and straightway loved an ass.

35 **Oberon.** This falls out better than I could devise.
But hast thou yet latched the Athenian's eyes
With the love juice, as I did bid thee do?

Robin. I took him sleeping—that is finished, too—
And the Athenian woman by his side,
40 That, when he waked, of force she must be eyed.

[Enter Demetrius and Hermia.]

Oberon. Stand close. This is the same Athenian.

Robin. This is the woman, but not this the man.

[They step aside.]

Demetrius. O, why rebuke you him that loves you so?
Lay breath so bitter on your bitter foe!

45 **Hermia.** Now I but chide, but I should use thee worse,
For thou, I fear, hast given me cause to curse.
If thou hast slain Lysander in his sleep,
Being o'er shoes in blood, plunge in the deep
And kill me too.
50 The sun was not so true unto the day
As he to me. Would he have stolen away
From sleeping Hermia? I'll believe as soon
This whole earth may be bored, and that the moon
May through the center creep and so displease
55 Her brother's noontide with th' Antipodes.
It cannot be but thou hast murdered him.
So should a murderer look, so dead, so grim.

Demetrius. So should the murdered look, and so should
I,
Pierced through the heart with your stern cruelty.
60 Yet you, the murderer, look as bright, as clear,
As yonder Venus in her glimmering sphere.

Hermia. What's this to my Lysander? Where is he?

69–70 Hermia wonders whether Demetrius killed the sleeping Lysander, having dared not confront him while he was awake. *Why does Hermia accuse Demetrius of murdering Lysander?*

70 *brave touch:* noble exploit (said ironically).

71 *worm:* serpent.

72–73 *for with . . . stung:* An adder never stung with a more forked tongue than yours.

74 *misprised:* mistaken.

78 *An if:* if; *therefor:* in return.

84–87 Demetrius says that his sorrow grows heavier due to lack of sleep. He compares sleep to a bankrupt person. Sleep will pay back a bit of the debt that it owes to sorrow if Demetrius waits here to receive sleep's offer *(tender).*

Ah, good Demetrius, wilt thou give him me?

Demetrius. I had rather give his carcass to my hounds.

65 **Hermia.** Out, dog! Out, cur! Thou driv'st me past the
    bounds
    Of maiden's patience. Hast thou slain him, then?
    Henceforth be never numbered among men.
    O, once tell true! Tell true, even for my sake!
    Durst thou have looked upon him, being awake?
70   And hast thou killed him sleeping? O brave touch!
    Could not a worm, an adder, do so much?
    An adder did it, for with doubler tongue
    Than thine, thou serpent, never adder stung.

Demetrius. You spend your passion on a misprised
    mood.
75   I am not guilty of Lysander's blood,
    Nor is he dead, for aught that I can tell.

Hermia. I pray thee, tell me then that he is well.

Demetrius. An if I could, what should I get therefor?

Hermia. A privilege never to see me more.
80   And from thy hated presence part I so.
    See me no more, whether he be dead or no.

[She exits.]

Demetrius. There is no following her in this fierce vein.
    Here, therefore, for a while I will remain.
    So sorrow's heaviness doth heavier grow
85   For debt that bankrout sleep doth sorrow owe,
    Which now in some slight measure it will pay,
    If for his tender here I make some stay.

[He lies down and falls asleep.]

Oberon *[to* Robin*].* What hast thou done? Thou hast
    mistaken quite
    And laid the love juice on some true-love's sight.

90 *Of thy misprision:* from your mistake; *perforce:* necessarily.

91 *turned:* changed.

92–93 Robin says that fate is responsible, since for every man who keeps his word there are a million who break promise after promise.

94 *About the wood go:* go through the wood.

95 *look thou:* be sure that you.

96 *fancy-sick:* lovesick; *cheer:* face.

97 In Shakespeare's time it was believed that sighs drain blood from the heart.

99 *against she do appear:* to prepare for her arrival.

101 The Tartar people of central Asia had bows more powerful than English ones.

107 *Venus:* the planet Venus.

109 *Beg of her for remedy:* beg her to relieve your love sickness.

113 *fee:* reward.

114 *fond pageant:* foolish spectacle.

119 *That must . . . alone:* That has to be unrivaled fun.

90　Of thy misprision must perforce ensue
　　Some true-love turned, and not a false turned true.

Robin. Then fate o'errules, that, one man holding
　　　troth,
　　A million fail, confounding oath on oath.

Oberon. About the wood go swifter than the wind,
95　And Helena of Athens look thou find.
　　All fancy-sick she is and pale of cheer
　　With sighs of love that costs the fresh blood dear.
　　By some illusion see thou bring her here.
　　I'll charm his eyes against she do appear.

100　**Robin.** I go, I go, look how I go,
　　Swifter than arrow from the Tartar's bow.

[He exits.]

Oberon *[applying the nectar to* Demetrius' *eyes].*
　　　　Flower of this purple dye,
　　　　Hit with Cupid's archery,
　　　　Sink in apple of his eye.
105　　　When his love he doth espy,
　　　　Let her shine as gloriously
　　　　As the Venus of the sky.
　　　　When thou wak'st, if she be by,
　　　　Beg of her for remedy.

[Enter Robin.*]*

110　**Robin.**　Captain of our fairy band,
　　　　　Helena is here at hand,
　　　　　And the youth, mistook by me,
　　　　　Pleading for a lover's fee.
　　　　　Shall we their fond pageant see?
115　　　　Lord, what fools these mortals be!

Oberon.　Stand aside. The noise they make
　　　　　Will cause Demetrius to awake.

Robin.　Then will two at once woo one.
　　　　　That must needs be sport alone.

121 *prepost'rously:* out of the natural order.

124–125 Lysander says that he weeps whenever he makes a vow, and vows made with tears are entirely truthful.

127 *badge of faith:* his tears.

128 *advance:* display.

129–133 Helena says that the truth of his vow to her kills the truth of his vow to Hermia. If he weighs one against the other, he will be weighing nothing, because the scales will be balanced evenly and because each vow has no more weight than a lie.

138 *eyne:* eyes.

139 *is muddy:* would be muddy in comparison; *show:* appearance.

141–143 Demetrius says that the pure frozen *(congealèd)* snow in the Taurus mountains seems black *(turns to a crow)* in comparison to the whiteness of her hand.

144 *This princess:* Helena's hand; *seal:* guarantee.

146 *set against:* attack.

148 *do me thus much injury:* insult me this way.

120   And those things do best please me
           That befall prepost'rously.

[They step aside.]

[Enter Lysander *and* Helena.*]*

Lysander. Why should you think that I should woo in
           scorn?
      Scorn and derision never come in tears.
      Look when I vow, I weep; and vows so born,
125   In their nativity all truth appears.
      How can these things in me seem scorn to you,
      Bearing the badge of faith to prove them true?

Helena. You do advance your cunning more and more.
      When truth kills truth, O devilish holy fray!
130   These vows are Hermia's. Will you give her o'er?
      Weigh oath with oath, and you will nothing weigh.
      Your vows to her and me, put in two scales,
      Will even weigh, and both as light as tales.

Lysander. I had no judgment when to her I swore.

135 **Helena.** Nor none, in my mind, now you give her o'er.

Lysander. Demetrius loves her, and he loves not you.

Demetrius *[waking up].* O Helen, goddess, nymph,
           perfect, divine!
      To what, my love, shall I compare thine eyne?
      Crystal is muddy. O, how ripe in show
140   Thy lips, those kissing cherries, tempting grow!
      That pure congealèd white, high Taurus' snow,
      Fanned with the eastern wind, turns to a crow
      When thou hold'st up thy hand. O, let me kiss
      This princess of pure white, this seal of bliss!

145 **Helena.** O spite! O hell! I see you all are bent
      To set against me for your merriment.
      If you were civil and knew courtesy,
      You would not do me thus much injury.
      Can you not hate me, as I know you do,

150 *join in souls:* unite.

153 *superpraise my parts:* overpraise my qualities. *How do you think Helena feels about having two suitors?*

157 *trim:* fine (said ironically).

158 *conjure:* bring.

159 *sort:* character.

160–161 *extort . . . patience:* torture the patience out of a poor soul.

161 *make you sport:* entertain yourselves.

165–167 *part:* share, claim; *bequeath:* hand over. *What is Lysander proposing to exchange with Demetrius?*

169 *I will none:* I want no part of her.

171 Demetrius claims that his heart only went to Hermia as a visitor.

175 *aby it dear:* pay dearly for it.

177–180 The night, which deprives the eyes of their function, makes our ears keener; to the extent that our sight is impaired, our hearing gets double compensation.

150 But you must join in souls to mock me too?
 If you were men, as men you are in show,
 You would not use a gentle lady so,
 To vow and swear and superpraise my parts,
 When, I am sure, you hate me with your hearts.
155 You both are rivals and love Hermia,
 And now both rivals to mock Helena.
 A trim exploit, a manly enterprise,
 To conjure tears up in a poor maid's eyes
 With your derision! None of noble sort
160 Would so offend a virgin and extort
 A poor soul's patience, all to make you sport.

Lysander. You are unkind, Demetrius. Be not so,
 For you love Hermia; this you know I know.
 And here with all goodwill, with all my heart,
165 In Hermia's love I yield you up my part.
 And yours of Helena to me bequeath,
 Whom I do love and will do till my death.

Helena. Never did mockers waste more idle breath.

Demetrius. Lysander, keep thy Hermia. I will none.
170 If e'er I loved her, all that love is gone.
 My heart to her but as guest-wise sojourned,
 And now to Helen is it home returned,
 There to remain.

Lysander.   Helen, it is not so.

Demetrius. Disparage not the faith thou dost not know,
175 Lest to thy peril thou aby it dear.
 Look where thy love comes. Yonder is thy dear.

[Enter Hermia.]

Hermia *[to Lysander].* Dark night, that from the eye his
  function takes,
 The ear more quick of apprehension makes;
 Wherein it doth impair the seeing sense,
180 It pays the hearing double recompense.

186 *bide:* wait, remain.

187 *engilds:* brightens.

188 *yon fiery . . . light:* those fiery stars.

193 *conjoined:* joined together.

194 *in spite of me:* to spite me.

196 *contrived:* schemed.

197 *bait me . . . derision:* torment me with this disgusting ridicule.

198 *counsel:* private discussion.

200 *chid:* scolded.

203 *artificial:* skillful.

206 *warbling . . . key:* both singing together in harmony.

208 *incorporate:* united in one body.

Thou art not by mine eye, Lysander, found;
Mine ear, I thank it, brought me to thy sound.
But why unkindly didst thou leave me so?

Lysander. Why should he stay whom love doth press
to go?

185 **Hermia.** What love could press Lysander from my
side?

Lysander. Lysander's love, that would not let him bide,
Fair Helena, who more engilds the night
Than all yon fiery oes and eyes of light.
Why seek'st thou me? Could not this make thee
know
190 The hate I bear thee made me leave thee so?

Hermia. You speak not as you think. It cannot be.

Helena. Lo, she is one of this confederacy!
Now I perceive they have conjoined all three
To fashion this false sport in spite of me.—
195 Injurious Hermia, most ungrateful maid,
Have you conspired, have you with these contrived,
To bait me with this foul derision?
Is all the counsel that we two have shared,
The sisters' vows, the hours that we have spent
200 When we have chid the hasty-footed time
For parting us—O, is all forgot?
All schooldays' friendship, childhood innocence?
We, Hermia, like two artificial gods,
Have with our needles created both one flower,
205 Both on one sampler, sitting on one cushion,
Both warbling of one song, both in one key,
As if our hands, our sides, voices, and minds
Had been incorporate. So we grew together
Like to a double cherry, seeming parted,
210 But yet an union in partition,
Two lovely berries molded on one stem;
So with two seeming bodies but one heart,

213–214 Helena uses the language of heraldry (**coats** of arms, **crest**) to describe how she and Hermia were joined together in unison.

215 *rent:* tear; *asunder:* apart.

218 *Our sex:* women in general.

225 *even but now:* until just now; *spurn:* kick.

226 *rare:* admirable.

227 *Wherefore:* why.

229 *Deny your love:* deny his love for you.

230 *tender:* offer; *forsooth:* in truth.

231 *setting on:* instigation, urging.

232 *What though:* what does it matter if; *grace:* favor.

237 *Persever:* persevere; *counterfeit sad looks:* pretend to look serious.

238 *Make mouths upon:* make faces at.

239 *hold . . . up:* keep up the sweet joke.

240 *carried:* managed; *chronicled:* recorded in history, famous.

242 *argument:* subject (of mockery).

Two of the first, like coats in heraldry,
Due but to one, and crownèd with one crest.
215 And will you rent our ancient love asunder,
To join with men in scorning your poor friend?
It is not friendly; 'tis not maidenly.
Our sex, as well as I, may chide you for it,
Though I alone do feel the injury.

220 **Hermia.** I am amazèd at your words.
I scorn you not. It seems that you scorn me.

Helena. Have you not set Lysander, as in scorn,
To follow me and praise my eyes and face,
And made your other love, Demetrius,
225 Who even but now did spurn me with his foot,
To call me goddess, nymph, divine and rare,
Precious, celestial? Wherefore speaks he this
To her he hates? And wherefore doth Lysander
Deny your love (so rich within his soul)
230 And tender me, forsooth, affection,
But by your setting on, by your consent?
What though I be not so in grace as you,
So hung upon with love, so fortunate,
But miserable most, to love unloved?
235 This you should pity rather than despise.

Hermia. I understand not what you mean by this.

Helena. Ay, do. Persever, counterfeit sad looks,
Make mouths upon me when I turn my back,
Wink each at other, hold the sweet jest up.
240 This sport, well carried, shall be chronicled.
If you have any pity, grace, or manners,
You would not make me such an argument.
But fare you well. 'Tis partly my own fault,
Which death or absence soon shall remedy.

245 **Lysander.** Stay, gentle Helena, Hear my excuse,
My love, my life, my soul, fair Helena.

Helena. O excellent!

249 Demetrius threatens to force Lysander to stop wooing Helena if Hermia's pleading fails to persuade him.

253 *by that . . . thee:* on my life.

254 Lysander challenges Demetrius to a duel.

257 *Whereto tends all this:* Where is all this leading?

258 *Ethiop:* Ethiopian (This seems to be a reference to the darkness of Hermia's hair or complexion.) *Why does Lysander insult Hermia?*

258–261 Demetrius taunts Lysander, accusing him of acting as if he's ready to go off and fight, but allowing Hermia to keep her hold on him.

264 *tawny:* tanned; *Tartar:* a person from central Asia (used here as an insult).

266 *sooth:* truly.

267 *my word:* my promise to duel.

Hermia *[to* Lysander*].* Sweet, do not scorn her so.

Demetrius *[to* Lysander*].* If she cannot entreat, I can
    compel.

250 **Lysander.** Thou canst compel no more than she entreat.
    Thy threats have no more strength than her weak
      prayers.
    Helen, I love thee. By my life, I do.
    I swear by that which I will lose for thee,
    To prove him false that says I love thee not.

255 **Demetrius.** I say I love thee more than he can do.

Lysander. If thou say so, withdraw and prove it too.

Demetrius. Quick, come.

Hermia.   Lysander, whereto tends all
    this?

[She takes hold of Lysander*.]*

Lysander. Away, you Ethiop!

Demetrius *[to* Hermia*].*   No, no. He'll
    Seem to break loose. *[To* Lysander*.]* Take on as you
      would follow,
260   But yet come not. You are a tame man, go!

Lysander *[to* Hermia*].* Hang off, thou cat, thou burr!
    Vile thing, let loose,
    Or I will shake thee from me like a serpent.

Hermia. Why are you grown so rude? What change is
    this,
    Sweet love?

Lysander.   Thy love? Out, tawny Tartar, out!
265   Out, loathèd med'cine! O, hated potion, hence!

Hermia. Do you not jest?

Helena.   Yes, sooth, and so do you.

Lysander. Demetrius, I will keep my word with thee.

268–269 Demetrius would like to have a signed agreement *(bond);* he doesn't trust Lysander's word because Hermia's arms *(a weak bond)* are capable of holding him back.

273 *Wherefore:* Why; *what news:* What has happened?

275 *erewhile:* formerly.

283 *juggler:* trickster; *cankerblossom:* cankerworm (a caterpillar that destroys flower blossoms).

291 *compare:* comparison.
292 *urged:* called attention to, presented favorably.
293 *personage:* stature.

Demetrius. I would I had your bond. For I perceive
    A weak bond holds you. I'll not trust your word.

270 **Lysander.** What? Should I hurt her, strike her, kill her
    dead?
    Although I hate her, I'll not harm her so.

Hermia. What, can you do me greater harm than hate?
    Hate me? Wherefore? O me, what news, my love?
    Am not I Hermia? Are not you Lysander?
275 I am as fair now as I was erewhile.
    Since night you loved me; yet since night you left me.
    Why, then, you left me—O, the gods forbid!—
    In earnest, shall I say?

Lysander.   Ay, by my life,
    And never did desire to see thee more.
280 Therefore be out of hope, of question, of doubt.
    Be certain, nothing truer, 'tis no jest
    That I do hate thee and love Helena.

[Hermia *turns him loose.*]

Hermia. O me! To Helena. You juggler, you
    cankerblossom,
    You thief of love! What, have you come by night
285 And stol'n my love's heart from him?

Helena.   Fine, i'faith.
    Have you no modesty, no maiden shame,
    No touch of bashfulness? What, will you tear
    Impatient answers from my gentle tongue?
    Fie, fie, you counterfeit, you puppet, you!
290 **Hermia.** "Puppet"? Why so? Ay, that way goes the
    game.
    Now I perceive that she hath made compare
    Between our statures; she hath urged her height,
    And with her personage, her tall personage,
    Her height, forsooth, she hath prevailed with him.
295 And are you grown so high in his esteem
    Because I am so dwarfish and so low?

297 *painted:* covered with make-up; *maypole:* tall, skinny person (literally, a pole around which people dance on May Day). *Why is Hermia so concerned about being shorter than Helena?*

301 *curst:* shrewish, quarrelsome.

303 *right maid:* real girl.

305 *something:* somewhat.

311 *stealth:* stealing away.

313 *chid me hence:* driven me away with his scolding.

315 *so:* if.

318 *fond:* foolish.

323 *though you take her part:* even if you take Hermia's side.

324 *keen and shrewd:* fierce and shrewish.

325 *vixen:* an ill-tempered female.

How low am I, thou painted maypole? Speak!
How low am I? I am not yet so low
But that my nails can reach unto thine eyes.

300 **Helena.** I pray you, though you mock me, gentlemen,
Let her not hurt me. I was never curst;
I have no gift at all in shrewishness.
I am a right maid for my cowardice.
Let her not strike me. You perhaps may think,
305 Because she is something lower than myself,
That I can match her.

Hermia.   "Lower"? Hark, again!

Helena. Good Hermia, do not be so bitter with me.
I evermore did love you, Hermia,
Did ever keep your counsels, never wronged you—
310 Save that, in love unto Demetrius,
I told him of your stealth unto this wood.
He followed you; for love, I followed him.
But he hath chid me hence and threatened me
To strike me, spurn me, nay, to kill me too.
315 And now, so you will let me quiet go,
To Athens will I bear my folly back
And follow you no further. Let me go.
You see how simple and how fond I am.

Hermia. Why, get you gone. Who is 't that hinders you?

320 **Helena.** A foolish heart that I leave here behind.

Hermia. What, with Lysander?

Helena.   With Demetrius.

Lysander. Be not afraid. She shall not harm thee,
Helena.

Demetrius. No, sir, she shall not, though you take her
part.

Helena. O, when she is angry, she is keen and shrewd.
325 She was a vixen when she went to school,

328 *suffer:* allow; ***flout me:*** treat me with contempt.

330 *minimus:* tiniest of creatures; ***knotgrass:*** a weed that was thought to stunt one's growth.

334–336 Demetrius threatens that if Lysander shows even the slightest love for Helena, he will pay for ***(aby)*** it.

336–338 Now that Hermia has stopped holding him, Lysander challenges Demetrius to follow him so they can fight over who has the most right to Helena.

339 ***cheek by jowl:*** side by side.

340 Hermia says that all this turmoil ***(coil)*** is on account of Helena.

346 *amazed:* bewildered.

347–348 ***Still thou . . . willfully:*** You always make mistakes, or else you do these tricks on purpose.

And though she be but little, she is fierce.

Hermia. "Little" again? Nothing but "low" and "little"?
Why will you suffer her to flout me thus?
Let me come to her.

Lysander.   Get you gone, you dwarf,
330   You minimus of hind'ring knotgrass made,
You bead, you acorn—

Demetrius.   You are too officious
In her behalf that scorns your services.
Let her alone. Speak not of Helena.
Take not her part. For if thou dost intend
335   Never so little show of love to her,
Thou shalt aby it.

Lysander.   Now she holds me not.
Now follow, if thou dar'st, to try whose right,
Of thine or mine, is most in Helena.

Demetrius. "Follow"? Nay, I'll go with thee, cheek by
jowl.

[Demetrius and Lysander exit.]

340   **Hermia.** You, mistress, all this coil is long of you.

[Helena retreats.]

Nay, go not back.

Helena. I will not trust you, I,
Nor longer stay in your curst company.
Your hands than mine are quicker for a fray.
345   My legs are longer though, to run away.

[She exits.]

Hermia. I am amazed and know not what to say.

[She exits.]

Oberon *[to Robin].* This is thy negligence. Still thou
mistak'st,

349 *shadows:* spirits.

354 *it so did sort:* it turned out this way.

355 *As . . . sport:* since I find their quarreling to be entertaining.

357–359 Oberon commands Robin to hurry *(Hie)* and immediately cover the sky *(welkin)* with a fog black as hell *(Acheron).*

361 *As:* that.

362 *Like . . . tongue:* sometimes imitate Lysander's voice.

363 *wrong:* insults.

364 *rail:* complain bitterly.

365 *look thou:* be sure that you.

367 *batty:* batlike.

368 *herb:* plant, flower.

368–371 Oberon orders him to anoint Lysander's eyes with the juice *(liquor)* of the plant, which is a powerful *(virtuous)* antidote that will restore Lysander's normal vision *(wonted sight).*

372 *derision:* ridiculous business.

373 *fruitless:* empty.

374 *wend:* make their way.

375 *With league . . . end:* in a union that will last until death.

381 *night's swift dragons:* the dragons that pull night's chariot across the sky.

Or else committ'st thy knaveries willfully.

Robin. Believe me, king of shadows, I mistook.
350 Did not you tell me I should know the man
By the Athenian garments he had on?
And so far blameless proves my enterprise
That I have 'nointed an Athenian's eyes;
And so far am I glad it so did sort,
355 As this their jangling I esteem a sport.

Oberon. Thou seest these lovers seek a place to fight.
Hie, therefore, Robin, overcast the night;
The starry welkin cover thou anon
With drooping fog as black as Acheron,
360 And lead these testy rivals so astray
As one come not within another's way.
Like to Lysander sometime frame thy tongue;
Then stir Demetrius up with bitter wrong.
And sometime rail thou like Demetrius.
365 And from each other look thou lead them thus,
Till o'er their brows death-counterfeiting sleep
With leaden legs and batty wings doth creep.
Then crush this herb into Lysander's eye,

[He gives the flower to Robin.]

Whose liquor hath this virtuous property,
370 To take from thence all error with his might
And make his eyeballs roll with wonted sight.
When they next wake, all this derision
Shall seem a dream and fruitless vision.
And back to Athens shall the lovers wend,
375 With league whose date till death shall never end.
Whiles I in this affair do thee employ,
I'll to my queen and beg her Indian boy;
And then I will her charmèd eye release
From monster's view, and all things shall be peace.

380 **Robin.** My fairy lord, this must be done with haste,
For night's swift dragons cut the clouds full fast,

382 ***Aurora's harbinger:*** Venus, the morning star, which announces the approach of dawn (Aurora).

384–385 ***Damnèd spirits . . . burial:*** The spirits are damned because these people committed suicide. Their bodies were either buried at crossroads (that is, unblessed ground) or left in the waters ***(floods)*** in which they drowned themselves.

389 ***For aye:*** forever.

390–397 Oberon says that unlike the damned spirits, they need not fear the morning. He has even walked about the woods until the sunrise made the ocean water turn golden. (However, he seems eager to avoid full daylight.)

401 ***Goblin:*** Hobgoblin (another name for Robin Goodfellow).

404 ***drawn:*** with drawn sword.

405 ***straight:*** right away.

406 ***plainer:*** flatter, more open.

And yonder shines Aurora's harbinger,
At whose approach, ghosts wand'ring here and
there
Troop home to churchyards. Damnèd spirits all,
385 That in crossways and floods have burial,
Already to their wormy beds are gone.
For fear lest day should look their shames upon,
They willfully themselves exile from light
And must for aye consort with black-browed night.

390 **Oberon.** But we are spirits of another sort.
I with the Morning's love have oft made sport
And, like a forester, the groves may tread
Even till the eastern gate, all fiery red,
Opening on Neptune with fair blessèd beams,
395 Turns into yellow gold his salt-green streams.
But notwithstanding, haste! Make no delay.
We may effect this business yet ere day.

[He exits.]

Robin. Up and down, up and down,
I will lead them up and down.
400 I am feared in field and town.
Goblin, lead them up and down.
Here comes one.

[Enter Lysander.*]*

Lysander. Where art thou, proud Demetrius? Speak
thou now.

Robin *[in* Demetrius' *voice].* Here, villain, drawn and
ready. Where art thou?
405 **Lysander.** I will be with thee straight.

Robin *[in* Demetrius' *voice].* Follow me, then, to plainer
ground.

[Lysander exits.*]*

[Enter Demetrius.*]*

412 *recreant:* coward.

413 Robin says that he will whip Demetrius with a rod; it would be shameful to use a sword on such a coward.

415 *try no manhood:* have no test of valor.

420 *That fallen . . . way:* so that I have come into a dark, unlevel place.

425 *Abide me:* wait for me; *wot:* know.

427 *stand:* face an attack.

Demetrius. Lysander, speak again.
　　Thou runaway, thou coward, art thou fled?
　　Speak! In some bush? Where dost thou hide thy
　　　head?

410 **Robin** [in Lysander's voice]. Thou coward, art thou
　　　bragging to the stars,
　　Telling the bushes that thou look'st for wars,
　　And wilt not come? Come, recreant! Come, thou
　　　child!
　　I'll whip thee with a rod. He is defiled
　　That draws a sword on thee.

Demetrius. 　　　　　　　　　Yea, art thou there?

415 **Robin** [in Lysander's voice]. Follow my voice. We'll try
　　no manhood here.

[They exit.]

[Enter Lysander.]

Lysander. He goes before me and still dares me on.
　　When I come where he calls, then he is gone.
　　The villain is much lighter-heeled than I.
　　I followed fast, but faster he did fly,
420　That fallen am I in dark uneven way,
　　And here will rest me. Come, thou gentle day,
　　For if but once thou show me thy gray light,
　　I'll find Demetrius and revenge this spite.

[He lies down and sleeps.]

[Enter Robin and Demetrius.]

Robin [in Lysander's voice]. Ho, ho, ho! Coward, why
　　com'st thou not?
425 **Demetrius.** Abide me, if thou dar'st, for well I wot
　　Thou runn'st before me, shifting every place,
　　And dar'st not stand nor look me in the face.
　　Where art thou now?

Robin [in Lysander's voice]. Come hither. I am here.

429 *buy this dear:* pay for this dearly.

431–432 *Faintness . . . bed:* Weakness forces me to sleep on the ground.

433 *look to be visited:* you can be sure I'll find you.

435 *Abate:* shorten.

437 *From . . . detest:* away from those who detest my company.

439 *Steal:* remove.

443 *curst:* angry.

447 *Bedabbled:* spattered.

451 *mean:* intend for there to be.

Demetrius. Nay, then, thou mock'st me. Thou shalt
    buy this dear
430   If ever I thy face by daylight see.
    Now go thy way. Faintness constraineth me
    To measure out my length on this cold bed.
    By day's approach look to be visited.

[He lies down and sleeps.]

[Enter Helena]

Helena. O weary night, O long and tedious night,
435   Abate thy hours! Shine, comforts, from the east,
    That I may back to Athens by daylight
     From these that my poor company detest.
    And sleep, that sometimes shuts up sorrow's eye,
    Steal me awhile from mine own company.
440   *[She lies down and sleeps.]*

Robin.   Yet but three? Come one more.
        Two of both kinds makes up four.
        Here she comes, curst and sad.
        Cupid is a knavish lad
445   Thus to make poor females mad.

[Enter Hermia]

Hermia. Never so weary, never so in woe,
     Bedabbled with the dew and torn with briers,
    I can no further crawl, no further go.
     My legs can keep no pace with my desires.
450   Here will I rest me till the break of day.
    Heavens shield Lysander if they mean a fray!

[She lies down and sleeps.]

Robin.   On the ground
        Sleep sound.
        I'll apply
455   To your eye,
      Gentle lover, remedy.

[Robin applies the nectar to Lysander's eyes.]

When thou wak'st,
Thou tak'st
True delight
In the sight
Of thy former lady's eye.
And the country proverb known,
That every man should take his own,
In your waking shall be shown.
Jack shall have Jill;
Naught shall go ill;
The man shall have his mare again, and all shall be
well.

[He exits.]

2 **While . . . coy:** while I caress your lovely cheeks.

FOUR

Scene 1 *The wood.*

Oberon watches as Titania entertains Bottom in her bower. She falls asleep with her arms wrapped around him. When Robin arrives, Oberon reveals that Titania has given him the Indian boy. He releases Titania from his spell and has Robin remove the ass's head from Bottom. After Titania casts a spell of deep sleep over Bottom and the Athenian lovers, she and Oberon exit with their followers.

Theseus, Hippolyta, and Egeus, who have come into the woods to celebrate May Day, find the four sleeping lovers. Lysander admits that he intended to elope with Hermia. Egeus demands that Lysander be punished, but Demetrius announces that he now wishes to marry Helena. Theseus invites both reunited couples to be married that day alongside Theseus and Hippolyta. They all depart for Athens, leaving Bottom still asleep in the woods. Finally, Bottom wakes up and marvels at the strange dream he had during the night.

[With the four lovers still asleep onstage, enter Titania, Queen of Fairies, *and* Bottom *and* Fairies, *and* Oberon, the King, *behind them unseen by those onstage.]*

Titania. Come, sit thee down upon this flow'ry bed,
    While I thy amiable cheeks do coy,
And stick muskroses in thy sleek smooth head,
    And kiss thy fair large ears, my gentle joy.

5 **Bottom.** Where's Peaseblossom?

Peaseblossom. Ready.

12–13 *Do not . . . action:* Do not wear yourself out too much.

18 *neaf:* fist.

19 Bottom may be telling Mustardseed to stop bowing or removing his hat out of respect.

21 *Cavalery:* Cavalier (a courtly term of address).

22 *Cobweb:* Probably an error for "Peaseblossom," since Cobweb has already been sent to bring honey.

23 *marvels:* marvelously.

27 *tongs and the bones:* instruments used in rustic music. (Tongs were struck by a piece of metal, like a triangle; bones were clappers held between the fingers.)

29 *peck of provender:* a quarter bushel of livestock feed.

31 *bottle:* bundle; *fellow:* equal.

Bottom. Scratch my head, Peaseblossom. Where's
    Monsieur Cobweb?

Cobweb. Ready.

Bottom. Monsieur Cobweb, good monsieur, get you
10   your weapons in your hand and kill me a red-hipped
    humble-bee on the top of a thistle, and, good mon-
    sieur, bring me the honey-bag. Do not fret yourself
    too much in the action, monsieur, and, good mon-
    sieur, have a care the honey-bag break not; I would be
15   loath to have you overflown with a honey-bag, signior.
    [Cobweb exits.] Where's Monsieur Mustardseed?

Mustardseed. Ready.

Bottom. Give me your neaf, Monsieur Mustardseed.
    Pray you, leave your courtesy, good monsieur.

20 **Mustardseed.** What's your will?

Bottom. Nothing, good monsieur, but to help Cavalery
    Cobweb to scratch. I must to the barber's, monsieur,
    for methinks I am marvels hairy about the face. And I
    am such a tender ass, if my hair do but tickle me, I
25   must scratch.

Titania. What, wilt thou hear some music, my sweet
    love?

Bottom. I have a reasonable good ear in music. Let's
    have the tongs and the bones.

Titania. Or say, sweet love, what thou desirest to eat.

Bottom. Truly, a peck of provender. I could munch your
30   good dry oats. Methinks I have a great desire to a
    bottle of hay. Good hay, sweet hay, hath no fellow.

Titania. I have a venturous fairy that shall seek
    The squirrel's hoard and fetch thee new nuts.

Bottom. I had rather have a handful or two of dried
35   peas. But, I pray you, let none of your people stir me;

36 exposition: Bottom's error for "disposition."

38 be all ways: scatter.

39 woodbine: a climbing plant.

41 Enrings: encircles.

44 dotage: foolish affection.

46 sweet favors: fragrant flowers.

50 sometime: formerly.
51 Was wont to: used to; **orient:** glowing, lustrous
52 flouriets: little flowers.

57 straight: immediately.

61 scalp: head.
62 swain: a country lad.
63 other: others.
64 May all . . . repair: All of them may return together to Athens.
65 accidents: happenings.

I have an exposition of sleep come upon me.

Titania. Sleep thou, and I will wind thee in my arms.—
Fairies, begone, and be all ways away.

[Fairies *exit.*]

So doth the woodbine the sweet honeysuckle
40 Gently entwist; the female ivy so
Enrings the barky fingers of the elm.
O, how I love thee! How I dote on thee!

[Bottom *and* Titania *sleep.*]

[*Enter* Robin Goodfellow.]

Oberon. Welcome, good Robin. Seest thou this sweet
sight?
Her dotage now I do begin to pity.
45 For, meeting her of late behind the wood,
Seeking sweet favors for this hateful fool,
I did upbraid her and fall out with her.
For she his hairy temples then had rounded
With coronet of fresh and fragrant flowers;
50 And that same dew, which sometime on the buds
Was wont to swell like round and orient pearls,
Stood now within the pretty flouriets' eyes,
Like tears that did their own disgrace bewail.
When I had at my pleasure taunted her,
55 And she in mild terms begged my patience,
I then did ask of her her changeling child,
Which straight she gave me, and her fairy sent
To bear him to my bower in Fairyland.
And now I have the boy, I will undo
60 This hateful imperfection of her eyes.
And, gentle Puck, take this transformèd scalp
From off the head of this Athenian swain,
That he, awaking when the other do,
May all to Athens back again repair
65 And think no more of this night's accidents

66 *vexation:* agitation

70 *Dian's bud:* Oberon's flower, which can release Titania from the spell, is associated with Diana, the goddess of chastity; it will undo the effects of love-in-idleness, the flower associated with Cupid.

76 *visage:* appearance.

78–79 Oberon asks her to put Bottom and the four lovers into an unusually deep sleep.

85 *solemnly:* ceremoniously.

86 *triumphantly:* in a festive procession.

But as the fierce vexation of a dream.
But first I will release the Fairy Queen.

[He applies the nectar to her eyes.]

Be as thou wast wont to be.
See as thou wast wont to see.
70   Dian's bud o'er Cupid's flower
Hath such force and blessèd power.
Now, my Titania, wake you, my sweet queen.

Titania [waking]. My Oberon, what visions have I seen!
Methought I was enamored of an ass.

75 **Oberon.** There lies your love.

Titania.   How came these things to
pass?
O, how mine eyes do loathe his visage now!

Oberon. Silence awhile.—Robin, take off this head.—
Titania, music call; and strike more dead
Than common sleep of all these five the sense.

80 **Titania.** Music, ho, music such as charmeth sleep!

Robin [removing the ass-head from Bottom]. Now, when
thou wak'st, with thine own fool's eyes peep.

Oberon. Sound music.

[Music.]

Come, my queen, take hands with
me,
And rock the ground whereon these sleepers be.

[Titania and Oberon dance.]

Now thou and I are new in amity,
85   And will tomorrow midnight solemnly
Dance in Duke Theseus' house triumphantly,
And bless it to all fair prosperity.
There shall the pairs of faithful lovers be
Wedded, with Theseus, all in jollity.

90 ***attend and mark:*** pay attention.

92–95 Oberon tells her that in silence they will walk rapidly after the night's shade; they can circle the earth more swiftly than the moon.

100 ***Wind horn:*** One or more hunting horns are blown.

101 ***Forester:*** the officer responsible for maintaining a forest.

102 ***observation:*** observance of May Day rites.

103 ***since we . . . day:*** since it still is morning.

104 ***music of my hounds:*** In Shakespeare's time, hunting dogs were appreciated for the musical quality of their barking.

105 ***uncouple:*** release the hounds.

108–109 ***mark the . . . conjunction:*** listen to the barking of the hounds together with their echoes from the mountains.

110 ***Cadmus:*** legendary founder of Thebes.

111 ***bayed:*** cut off from escape.

112 ***hounds of Sparta:*** a hunting breed admired in antiquity

113 ***chiding:*** barking.

118 ***So flewed, so sanded:*** with the same folds of flesh at the sides of their jaws and the same sandy coloring.

120 ***dewlapped:*** with folds of loose skin at the throat.

90 **Robin.** Fairy king, attend and mark.
       I do hear the morning lark.

Oberon. Then, my queen, in silence sad
         Trip we after night's shade.
         We the globe can compass soon,
95   Swifter than the wand'ring moon.

Titania. Come, my lord, and in our flight
          Tell me how it came this night
          That I sleeping here was found
          With these mortals on the ground.

[Oberon, Robin, and Titania exit.]

100 *[Wind horn. Enter Theseus and all his train, Hippolyta, Egeus.]*

Theseus. Go, one of you, find out the Forester.
         For now our observation is performed,
         And, since we have the vaward of the day,
         My love shall hear the music of my hounds.
105   Uncouple in the western valley; let them go.
         Dispatch, I say, and find the Forester.

[A Servant exits.]

         We will, fair queen, up to the mountain's top
         And mark the musical confusion
         Of hounds and echo in conjunction.

110 **Hippolyta.** I was with Hercules and Cadmus once,
          When in a wood of Crete they bayed the bear
          With hounds of Sparta. Never did I hear
          Such gallant chiding, for, besides the groves,
          The skies, the fountains, every region near
115   Seemed all one mutual cry. I never heard
          So musical a discord, such sweet thunder.

Theseus. My hounds are bred out of the Spartan kind,
         So flewed, so sanded; and their heads are hung
         With ears that sweep away the morning dew;
120   Crook-kneed, and dewlapped like Thessalian bulls;

A Midsummer Night's Dream **121**

121–122 *matched in . . . each:* The hounds were chosen for their harmonious barking, like a set of bells arranged according to note.

122 *cry:* a pack of hounds; *tunable:* well-tuned, harmonious.

125 *soft:* wait a moment.

129 *of:* at.

132 *in grace of our solemnity:* to honor our ceremony.

137–138 Birds were supposed to choose their mates on St. Valentine's Day.

143 *jealousy:* suspicion.

145 *amazèdly:* in a state of bewilderment.

Slow in pursuit, but matched in mouth like bells,
Each under each. A cry more tunable
Was never hollowed to, nor cheered with horn,
In Crete, in Sparta, nor in Thessaly.
125 Judge when you hear.—But soft! What nymphs are
these?

Egeus. My lord, this is my daughter here asleep,
And this Lysander; this Demetrius is,
This Helena, old Nedar's Helena.
I wonder of their being here together.

130 **Theseus.** No doubt they rose up early to observe
The rite of May, and hearing our intent,
Came here in grace of our solemnity.
But speak, Egeus. Is not this the day
That Hermia should give answer of her choice?

135 **Egeus.** It is, my lord.

Theseus. Go, bid the huntsmen wake them with their
horns.

[A Servant *exits.*]

[*Shout within. Wind horns. They all start up.*]

Theseus. Good morrow, friends. Saint Valentine is past.
Begin these woodbirds but to couple now?

[Demetrius, Helena, Hermia, *and* Lysander *kneel.*]

140 **Lysander.** Pardon, my lord.

Theseus.   I pray you all, stand up.

[*They rise.*]

I know you two are rival enemies.
How comes this gentle concord in the world,
That hatred is so far from jealousy
To sleep by hate and fear no enmity?

145 **Lysander.** My lord, I shall reply amazèdly,
Half sleep, half waking. But as yet, I swear,

148 ***truly would I speak:*** I wish to speak the truth. *How does this speech give the impression of someone who has just woken up?*

152 ***Without the peril:*** outside of, beyond.

156 ***defeated:*** defrauded.

161 ***hither:*** in coming here.

162 ***fancy:*** love.

163 ***wot:*** know.

166 ***idle gaud:*** worthless trinket.

168 ***virtue:*** power.

172 ***like a sickness:*** like one who is sick.

177 ***anon:*** soon.

178 ***overbear:*** overrule.

181 ***for:*** since; ***something:*** somewhat.

I cannot truly say how I came here.
But, as I think—for truly would I speak,
And now I do bethink me, so it is:
150   I came with Hermia hither. Our intent
Was to be gone from Athens, where we might,
Without the peril of the Athenian law—

Egeus. Enough, enough!—My lord, you have enough.
I beg the law, the law, upon his head.
155   They would have stol'n away.—They would, Demetrius,
Thereby to have defeated you and me:
You of your wife and me of my consent,
Of my consent that she should be your wife.

Demetrius. My lord, fair Helen told me of their stealth,
160   Of this their purpose hither to this wood,
And I in fury hither followed them,
Fair Helena in fancy following me.
But, my good lord, I wot not by what power
(But by some power it is) my love to Hermia,
165   Melted as the snow, seems to me now
As the remembrance of an idle gaud
Which in my childhood I did dote upon,
And all the faith, the virtue of my heart,
The object and the pleasure of mine eye,
170   Is only Helena. To her, my lord,
Was I betrothed ere I saw Hermia.
But like a sickness did I loathe this food.
But, as in health, come to my natural taste,
Now I do wish it, love it, long for it,
175   And will forevermore be true to it.

Theseus. Fair lovers, you are fortunately met.
Of this discourse we more will hear anon.—
Egeus, I will overbear your will,
For in the temple by and by, with us,
180   These couples shall eternally be knit.—
And, for the morning now is something worn,
Our purposed hunting shall be set aside.
Away with us to Athens. Three and three,

184 *in great solemnity:* with great ceremony.

188 *with parted eye:* with eyes out of focus.

190–191 *like a . . . own:* like a jewel that one finds but cannot be sure of keeping.

201 *Hey-ho:* a call to his fellow laborers.

202 *God's my life:* God save me! (an exclamation of surprise).

205–206 *Man is . . . dream:* Only an ass would try to explain this dream.

208 *patched:* that is, wearing motley (Fools often dressed in a coat of various colors.)

We'll hold a feast in great solemnity.
185   Come, Hippolyta.

[*Theseus and his train, including* Hippolyta *and* Egeus, *exit.*]

Demetrius. These things seem small and undistinguish-
     able,
Like far-off mountains turnèd into clouds.

Hermia. Methinks I see these things with parted eye,
When everything seems double.

Helena.   So methinks.
190   And I have found Demetrius like a jewel,
Mine own and not mine own.

Demetrius.   Are you sure
That we are awake? It seems to me
That yet we sleep, we dream. Do not you think
The Duke was here and bid us follow him?
195   **Hermia.** Yea, and my father.

Helena.   And Hippolyta.

Lysander. And he did bid us follow to the temple.

Demetrius. Why, then, we are awake. Let's follow him,
And by the way let us recount our dreams.

[*Lovers exit.*]

Bottom [*waking up*]. When my cue comes, call me, and
200   I will answer. My next is "Most fair Pyramus."
Hey-ho! Peter Quince! Flute the bellows-mender!
Snout the tinker! Starveling! God's my life! Stolen
hence and left me asleep! I have had a most rare
vision. I have had a dream past the wit of man to
205   say what dream it was. Man is but an ass if he go
about to expound this dream. Methought I was—
there is no man can tell what. Methought I was
and methought I had—but man is but a patched
fool if he will offer to say what methought I had.
210   The eye of man hath not heard, the ear of man

210–214 Bottom attempts to paraphrase a passage in the Bible (1 Corinthians 2:9): "The eye hath not seen, and the ear hath not heard, neither hath entered into the heart of man. . . ." He mixes up the functions of the sense organs.

215 *hath no bottom:* is too deep for human understanding.

218 *her:* Thisbe's.

2 *Out of doubt:* without a doubt; *transported:* carried off.

4 *discharge:* play, perform.

5 *wit:* intellect.

6 *person:* appearance; *paramour:* the lover of a married person.

7 *a thing of naught:* a shameful thing.

hath not seen, man's hand is not able to taste, his
tongue to conceive, nor his heart to report what
my dream was. I will get Peter Quince to write a
ballad of this dream. It shall be called "Bottom's
215   Dream" because it hath no bottom; and I will sing
it in the latter end of a play, before the Duke.
Peradventure, to make it the more gracious, I shall
sing it at her death.

[He exits.]

Scene 2 *Athens.*

*With no sign of Bottom, the craftsmen fear that the
performance must be canceled. Then Bottom arrives. He
announces that their play has been chosen for the
wedding festivities.*

[Enter Quince, Flute, Snout, and Starveling.]

Quince. Have you sent to Bottom's house? Is he come
home yet?

Starveling. He cannot be heard of. Out of doubt he is
transported.

Flute. If he come not, then the play is marred. It goes
not forward, doth it?

Quince. It is not possible. You have not a man in all
Athens able to discharge Pyramus but he.

5   **Flute.** No, he hath simply the best wit of any handi-
craftman in Athens.

Quince. Yea, and the best person too, and he is a very
paramour for a sweet voice.

Flute. You must say "paragon." A "paramour" is
(God bless us) a thing of naught.

[Enter Snug the joiner.]

10–11 *we had . . . men:* we would have had our fortunes made.

12–13 *six pence . . . life:* Flute's estimate of the royal pension Bottom would have received.

14 *An:* if.

18 *hearts:* good-hearted fellows.

19 *courageous:* splendid.

20–22 *am to discourse wonders:* have wonders to tell about; *right as it fell out:* exactly as it happened. *How much of the night's events do you think Bottom remembers?*

24 *of me:* out of me.

26 *strings:* strings for attaching false beards.

26–27 *ribbons to your pumps:* Actors' shoes were often decorated with ribbons; *presently:* right away.

29 *preferred:* put on the list of available entertainments.

Snug. Masters, the Duke is coming from the temple, and there is two or three lords and ladies more
10 married. If our sport had gone forward, we had all been made men.

Flute. O, sweet bully Bottom! Thus hath he lost six pence a day during his life. He could not have 'scaped six pence a day. An the Duke had not given
15 him six pence a day for playing Pyramus, I'll be hanged. He would have deserved it. Six pence a day in Pyramus, or nothing!

[Enter Bottom.]

Bottom. Where are these lads? Where are these hearts?

Quince. Bottom! O most courageous day! O most happy hour!

20 **Bottom.** Masters, I am to discourse wonders. But ask me not what; for, if I tell you, I am not true Athenian. I will tell you everything right as it fell out.

Quince. Let us hear, sweet Bottom.

Bottom. Not a word of me. All that I will tell you is
25 that the Duke hath dined. Get your apparel together, good strings to your beards, new ribbons to your pumps. Meet presently at the palace. Every man look o'er his part. For the short and the long is, our play is preferred. In any case, let Thisbe have
30 clean linen, and let not him that plays the lion pare his nails, for they shall hang out for the lion's claws. And, most dear actors, eat no onions nor garlic, for we are to utter sweet breath, and I do not doubt but to hear them say it is a sweet comedy. No more
35 words. Away! Go, away!

[They exit.]

1 **that:** that which, what.

2 **may:** can.

3 **antique:** old, strange; **fairy toys:** foolish tales about fairies.

5 **shaping fantasies:** creative imaginations; **apprehend:** imagine.

6 **comprehends:** understands.

8 **of imagination all compact:** entirely made up of imagination.

10 **all as frantic:** just as insane.

11 **Sees Helen's . . . Egypt:** Sees Helen of Troy's beauty in a Gypsy's face.

ACT FIVE

Scene 1 *The palace of Theseus.*

Theseus tells Hippolyta that he doesn't believe the stories told about the previous night, noting that lovers tend to have overactive imaginations. When the other newlyweds arrive, he asks what entertainment is available and chooses a play about Pyramus and Thisbe, despite being warned that the speeches and the actors are inept. The craftsmen amuse Theseus and his guests with an absurdly bad performance. After the play is concluded, the couples go off to bed. Oberon and Titania enter with their followers to bless each marriage. In an epilogue, Robin asks the audience to excuse the play's shortcomings by thinking of it as a dream.

[Enter Theseus, Hippolyta, *and* Philostrate, Lords, *and* Attendants.*]*

Hippolyta. 'Tis strange, my Theseus, that these lovers
    speak of.

Theseus. More strange than true. I never may believe
    These antique fables, nor these fairy toys.
    Lovers and madmen have such seething brains,
5   Such shaping fantasies, that apprehend
    More than cool reason ever comprehends.
    The lunatic, the lover, and the poet
    Are of imagination all compact.
    One sees more devils than vast hell can hold:
10   That is the madman. The lover, all as frantic,
    Sees Helen's beauty in a brow of Egypt.
    The poet's eye, in a fine frenzy rolling,
    Doth glance from heaven to earth, from earth to

12–18 Theseus describes how the poet, in a state of creative frenzy, writes concrete descriptions of things that cannot be known through the senses.

19–20 *if it . . . joy:* If it only imagines some joy, it perceives someone who brought that joy.

21 *some fear:* something to be afraid of.

23–27 Hippolyta says that the story of the previous night is too consistent to be merely a product of their imaginations, although it is strange and surprising. *Why do you think Hippolyta is more willing to believe the lovers' story than Theseus is?*

30–31 *More than . . . bed:* May even more joy than ours await you in your walks, at your table, and in your bed.

32 *masques:* elaborate court performances that included dialogue, singing, and dancing.

34 *after-supper:* a light meal or dessert.

36 *revels:* court entertainments.

39 *abridgment:* pastime (to abridge or shorten the evening).

heaven,
And as imagination bodies forth
15 The forms of things unknown, the poet's pen
Turns them to shapes and gives to airy nothing
A local habitation and a name.
Such tricks hath strong imagination
That, if it would but apprehend some joy,
20 It comprehends some bringer of that joy.
Or in the night, imagining some fear,
How easy is a bush supposed a bear!

Hippolyta. But all the story of the night told over,
And all their minds transfigured so together,
25 More witnesseth than fancy's images
And grows to something of great constancy,
But, howsoever, strange and admirable.

[Enter Lovers: Lysander, Demetrius, Hermia, *and* Helena.*]*

Theseus. Here come the lovers full of joy and mirth.—
Joy, gentle friends! Joy and fresh days of love
30 Accompany your hearts!

Lysander. More than to us
Wait in your royal walks, your board, your bed!

Theseus. Come now, what masques, what dances shall
we have
To wear away this long age of three hours
Between our after-supper and bedtime?
35 Where is our usual manager of mirth?
What revels are in hand? Is there no play
To ease the anguish of a torturing hour?
Call Philostrate.

Philostrate *[coming forward]*
Here, mighty Theseus.

Theseus. Say what abridgment have you for this
evening,
40 What masque, what music? How shall we beguile
The lazy time if not with some delight?

A Midsummer Night's Dream 135

42 *brief:* a list; sports: entertainments; *ripe:* ready to be presented.

44–47 According to Plutarch's "Life of Theseus," Hercules and Theseus were cousins. Theseus rejects a ballad about the battle between Hercules and the centaurs, a race of monsters. A centaur had the head, arms, and trunk of a man and legs of a horse.

49–50 Orpheus *(the Thracian singer)* was torn to pieces by worshipers *(Bacchanals)* of Bacchus, the god of wine.

50 *device:* show, entertainment.

52–53 *The thrice-three . . . beggary:* a satire about the neglect of learning and the impoverishment of scholars. (The nine *Muses* were goddesses who presided over literature and the arts and sciences.)

55 *sorting with:* suitable for.

74 *toiled:* burdened; *unbreathed:* unexercised.

Philostrate [*giving* Theseus *a paper*]. There is a brief
　　　how many sports are ripe.
　　Make choice of which your Highness will see first.

Theseus. "The battle with the Centaurs, to be sung
45　　By an Athenian eunuch to the harp."
　　We'll none of that. That have I told my love
　　In glory of my kinsman Hercules.
　　"The riot of the tipsy Bacchanals,
　　Tearing the Thracian singer in their rage."
50　　That is an old device, and it was played
　　When I from Thebes came last a conqueror.
　　"The thrice-three Muses mourning for the death
　　Of learning, late deceased in beggary."
　　That is some satire, keen and critical,
55　　Not sorting with a nuptial ceremony.
　　"A tedious brief scene of young Pyramus
　　And his love Thisbe, very tragical mirth."
　　"Merry" and "tragical"? "Tedious" and "brief"?
　　That is hot ice and wondrous strange snow!
60　　How shall we find the concord of this discord?

Philostrate. A play there is, my lord, some ten words
　　　long
　　(Which is as brief as I have known a play),
　　But by ten words, my lord, it is too long,
　　Which makes it tedious; for in all the play,
65　　There is not one word apt, one player fitted.
　　And tragical, my noble lord, it is.
　　For Pyramus therein doth kill himself,
　　Which, when I saw rehearsed, I must confess,
　　Made mine eyes water; but more merry tears
70　　The passion of loud laughter never shed.

Theseus. What are they that do play it?

Philostrate. Hard-handed men that work in Athens
　　　here,
　　Which never labored in their minds till now,
　　And now have toiled their unbreathed memories

75 *against:* in preparation for.

80 *stretched:* strained; *conned:* memorized.

83 *simpleness:* sincerity.

85–86 Hippolyta objects that she doesn't like to see poor people overburdened *(wretchedness o'ercharged)* or duty perishing in its attempt to serve.

88 *in this kind:* in this kind of thing (i.e., acting).

90 *take:* accept.

91–92 *noble respect . . . merit:* The noble view is to consider the effort made rather than the quality of achievement. *What traits of Theseus are revealed in this speech?*

93 *come:* journeyed; *clerks:* scholars.

94 *premeditated welcomes:* welcome speeches planned in advance.

96 *Make periods:* stop or stammer.

97 *Throttle . . . accent:* strangle the delivery they had rehearsed.

98 *dumbly:* silently.

105 *in least:* in saying least; *to my capacity:* in my opinion.

75   With this same play, against your nuptial.

Theseus. And we will hear it.

Philostrate.   No, my noble lord,
    It is not for you. I have heard it over,
    And it is nothing, nothing in the world,
    Unless you can find sport in their intents,
80   Extremely stretched and conned with cruel pain
    To do you service.

Theseus.   I will hear that play,
    For never anything can be amiss
    When simpleness and duty tender it.
    Go, bring them in—and take your places, ladies.

[Philostrate exits.]

85 **Hippolyta.** I love not to see wretchedness o'ercharged,
    And duty in his service perishing.

Theseus. Why, gentle sweet, you shall see no such thing.

Hippolyta. He says they can do nothing in this kind.

Theseus. The kinder we, to give them thanks for nothing.
90   Our sport shall be to take what they mistake;
    And what poor duty cannot do, noble respect
    Takes it in might, not merit.
    Where I have come, great clerks have purposèd
    To greet me with premeditated welcomes,
95   Where I have seen them shiver and look pale,
    Make periods in the midst of sentences,
    Throttle their practiced accent in their fears,
    And in conclusion dumbly have broke off,
    Not paying me a welcome. Trust me, sweet,
100   Out of this silence yet I picked a welcome,
    And in the modesty of fearful duty,
    I read as much as from the rattling tongue
    Of saucy and audacious eloquence.
    Love, therefore, and tongue-tied simplicity
105   In least speak most, to my capacity.

106 *Prologue:* the speaker of the prologue; ***addressed:*** ready to begin.

108–117 The punctuation indicates that Quince pauses in the wrong places, thereby turning a cautiously respectful speech into an absurd and even insulting one.

111 *end:* purpose.

113 *minding:* intending.

118 ***doth not stand upon points:*** does not care much about details, ignores punctuation.

119 *rid:* ridden; ***rough:*** untrained.

120 ***the stop:*** punctuation mark (literally, a term for bringing a galloping horse to a halt).

123 *recorder:* a flutelike wind instrument.; ***government:*** control.

124 *nothing:* not at all.

[Enter Philostrate.]

Philostrate. So please your Grace, the Prologue is
   addressed.

Theseus. Let him approach.

[Enter the Prologue.]

Prologue. If we offend, it is with our goodwill.
   That you should think we come not to offend,
110   But with goodwill. To show our simple skill,
   That is the true beginning of our end.
   Consider, then, we come but in despite.
   We do not come, as minding to content you,
   Our true intent is. All for your delight
115   We are not here. That you should here repent you,
   The actors are at hand, and, by their show,
   You shall know all that you are like to know.

[Prologue exits.]

Theseus. This fellow doth not stand upon points.

Lysander. He hath rid his prologue like a rough colt;
120   he knows not the stop. A good moral, my lord: it is
   not enough to speak, but to speak true.

Hippolyta. Indeed he hath played on this prologue like a
   child on a recorder—a sound, but not in government.

Theseus. His speech was like a tangled chain—nothing
125   impaired, but all disordered. Who is next?

*[Enter Pyramus (Bottom), and Thisbe (Flute), and Wall (Snout),
and Moonshine (Starveling), and Lion (Snug), and Prologue
(Quince).]*

Quince *[as Prologue].* Gentles, perchance you wonder at
   this show.
   But wonder on, till truth make all things plain.
   This man is Pyramus, if you would know.
   This beauteous lady Thisbe is certain.

131 *sunder:* separate.

133 *at the . . . wonder:* Let no one wonder what they whispered about.

136 *think no scorn:* think it no disgrace.

138 *hight:* is called.

141 *fall:* drop.

143 *tall:* handsome, elegant.

146 *broached:* stabbed.

147 *tarrying . . . shade:* having waited for him in the shade of a mulberry tree.

150 *At large discourse:* communicate at length.

153 *interlude:* play.

161 *sinister:* left.

130   This man with lime and roughcast doth present
        "Wall," that vile wall which did these lovers
        sunder;
    And through Wall's chink, poor souls, they are con-
    tent
        To whisper, at the which let no man wonder.
    This man, with lantern, dog, and bush of thorn,
135   Presenteth "Moonshine," for, if you will know,
    By moonshine did these lovers think no scorn
        To meet at Ninus' tomb, there, there to woo.
    This grisly beast (which "Lion" hight by name)
        The trusty Thisbe coming first by night
140   Did scare away, or rather did affright;
    And, as she fled, her mantle she did fall,
        Which Lion vile with bloody mouth did stain.
    Anon comes Pyramus, sweet youth and tall,
        And finds his trusty Thisbe's mantle slain.
145   Whereat, with blade, with bloody blameful blade,
        He bravely broached his boiling bloody breast.
    And Thisbe, tarrying in mulberry shade,
        His dagger drew, and died. For all the rest,
    Let Lion, Moonshine, Wall, and lovers twain
150   At large discourse, while here they do remain.

Theseus. I wonder if the lion be to speak.

Demetrius. No wonder, my lord. One lion may when
    many asses do.

[Lion, Thisbe, Moonshine, and Prologue *exit.]*

Snout *[as Wall].* In this same interlude it doth befall
    That I, one Snout by name, present a wall;
155   And such a wall as I would have you think
    That had in it a crannied hole or chink,
    Through which the lovers, Pyramus and Thisbe,
    Did whisper often, very secretly.
    This loam, this roughcast, and this stone doth show
160   That I am that same wall. The truth is so.
    And this the cranny is, right and sinister,

163 *lime and hair:* materials used to make plaster.

164 *wittiest:* most intelligent.

166 *grim-looked:* grim-looking.

173 *blink:* peer.; *eyne:* eyes.

174 *Thanks:* in response to Wall making a chink with his fingers; *Jove shield thee:* God protect you.

178 *sensible:* sensitive, capable of feeling; *curse again:* return the curse.

181 *fall pat:* happen exactly.

Through which the fearful lovers are to whisper.

Theseus. Would you desire lime and hair to speak better?

Demetrius. It is the wittiest partition that ever I heard discourse, my lord.

165 **Theseus.** Pyramus draws near the wall. Silence.

Bottom *[as Pyramus]*.
O grim-looked night! O night with hue so black!
O night, which ever art when day is not!
O night! O night! Alack, alack, alack!
I fear my Thisbe's promise is forgot.
170 And thou, O wall, O sweet, O lovely wall,
That stand'st between her father's ground and mine,
Thou wall, O wall, O sweet and lovely wall,
Show me thy chink to blink through with mine eyne.
Thanks, courteous wall. Jove shield thee well for this.
175 But what see I? No Thisbe do I see.
O wicked wall, through whom I see no bliss,
Cursed be thy stones for thus deceiving me!

Theseus. The wall, methinks, being sensible, should curse again.

Bottom. No, in truth, sir, he should not. "Deceiving me"
180 is Thisbe's cue. She is to enter now, and I am to spy
her through the wall. You shall see it will fall pat
as I told you. Yonder she comes.

[Enter Thisbe (Flute).*]*

Flute *[as Thisbe]*.
O wall, full often hast thou heard my moans
For parting my fair Pyramus and me.
185 My cherry lips have often kissed thy stones,
Thy stones with lime and hair knit up in thee.

Bottom *[as Pyramus]*.

188 *To spy an:* to see if.

191 *lover's grace:* gracious lover.

192–193 *Limander, Helen:* errors for "Leander" and "Hero," famous lovers in classical mythology.

194 *Shafalus, Procrus:* errors for "Cephalus" and "Procris." (In classical mythology, Cephalus remained faithful to his wife, Procris, after being abducted by the goddess of the morning.) *Why do your think Bottom makes so many mistakes?*

198 *Ninny's:* Ninus's.

199 *'Tide life, 'tide death:* come (betide) life or death.

200 *dischargèd:* performed.

203–204 *are so . . . warning:* are so eager to hear without giving the parents warning (a joking reference to the proverbial saying, "Walls have ears").

I see a voice! Now will I to the chink
   To spy an I can hear my Thisbe's face.
Thisbe?

190 **Flute** [as Thisbe]. My love! Thou art my love, I think.

Bottom [as Pyramus].
   Think what thou wilt, I am thy lover's grace,
   And, like Limander, am I trusty still.

Flute [as Thisbe].
   And I like Helen, till the Fates me kill.

Bottom [as Pyramus].
   Not Shafalus to Procrus was so true.

Flute [as Thisbe].
195   As Shafalus to Procrus, I to you.

Bottom [as Pyramus].
   O kiss me through the hole of this vile wall.

Flute [as Thisbe].
   I kiss the wall's hole, not your lips at all.

Bottom [as Pyramus].
   Wilt thou at Ninny's tomb meet me straightway?

Flute [as Thisbe].
   'Tide life, 'tide death, I come without delay.

[Bottom and Flute exit.]

Snout [as Wall].
200   Thus have I, Wall, my part dischargèd so,
   And, being done, thus Wall away doth go.

[He exits.]

Theseus. Now is the wall down between the two
   neighbors.

Demetrius. No remedy, my lord, when walls are so
   willful to hear without warning.

Hippolyta. This is the silliest stuff that ever I heard.

205 *in this kind:* of this sort (that is, plays); ***but shadows:*** merely illusions.

210–215 Snug reassures the audience that he is only a man playing the part of a lion. ***fell:*** fierce; ***dam:*** mother.

217 *'twere pity on my life:* it would be a pity that I should live.

220–224 These are backhanded compliments: foxes are known for slyness rather than valor and geese for foolishness rather than discretion.

227 *lanthorn:* lantern; ***hornèd moon:*** crescent moon.

Theseus. The best in this kind are but shadows, and the worst are no worse, if imagination amend them.

Hippolyta. It must be your imagination, then, and not theirs.

Theseus. If we imagine no worse of them than they of themselves, they may pass for excellent men. Here come two noble beasts in, a man and a lion.

[Enter Lion (Snug) *and* Moonshine (Starveling).*]*

Snug *[as* Lion*].*

You ladies, you whose gentle hearts do fear
The smallest monstrous mouse that creeps on floor,
May now perchance both quake and tremble here,
When lion rough in wildest rage doth roar.
Then know that I, as Snug the joiner, am
A lion fell, nor else no lion's dam;
For if I should as lion come in strife
Into this place, 'twere pity on my life.

Theseus. A very gentle beast, and of a good conscience.

Demetrius. The very best at a beast, my lord, that e'er I saw.

Lysander. This lion is a very fox for his valor.

Theseus. True, and a goose for his discretion.

Demetrius. Not so, my lord, for his valor cannot carry his discretion, and the fox carries the goose.

Theseus. His discretion, I am sure, cannot carry his valor, for the goose carries not the fox. It is well. Leave it to his discretion, and let us listen to the Moon.

Starveling *[as* Moonshine*].* This lanthorn doth the

228 Demetrius jokingly alludes to the horns of a cuckold (a man whose wife is unfaithful).

229 *no crescent:* not a crescent moon.

235 *for the candle:* because of the candle.

236 *in snuff:* angry, resentful (literally, in need of having its wick trimmed).

244–247 See note for Act 3, scene 1, lines 58–59.

hornèd moon present.

Demetrius. He should have worn the horns on his head.

Theseus. He is no crescent, and his horns are invisible within the circumference.

230 **Starveling** [as Moonshine]. This lanthorn doth the
hornèd moon present.
Myself the man i' th' moon do seem to be.

Theseus. This is the greatest error of all the rest; the man should be put into the lanthorn. How is it else "the man i' th' moon"?

235 **Demetrius.** He dares not come there for the candle, for you see, it is already in snuff.

Hippolyta. I am aweary of this moon. Would he would change.

Theseus. It appears by his small light of discretion that he is in the wane; but yet, in courtesy, in all reason, we must stay the time.

240 **Lysander.** Proceed, Moon.

Starveling [as Moonshine]. All that I have to say is to tell you that the lanthorn is the moon, I the man i' th' moon, this thornbush my thornbush, and this dog my dog.

245 **Demetrius.** Why, all these should be in the lanthorn, for all these are in the moon. But silence. Here comes Thisbe.

[Enter Thisbe (Flute).]

Flute [as Thisbe]. This is old Ninny's tomb. Where is my love?

Snug [as Lion]. O!

[The Lion roars. Thisbe runs off, dropping her mantle.]

250 **Demetrius.** Well roared, Lion.

253 *moused:* shaken, torn (as a cat treats a mouse).

262 *dole:* sorrow.

268 *Furies:* avenging goddesses of classical mythology; *fell:* fierce.

269 *Fates:* the three goddesses who spin, draw out, and cut the thread of human life.

270 *Cut thread and thrum:* Cut everything. (The thrum is the tufted end of thread left in a loom after the woven cloth is cut out.)

271 *Quail:* overpower; *quell:* kill.

272–273 *What point is Theseus making with this remark about Bottom's outburst of strong emotion* **(passion)?**

273 *Beshrew:* curse.

274 *Wherefore:* why; *frame:* create.

275 *deflowered:* ravished, disfigured.

Theseus. Well run, Thisbe.

Hippolyta. Well shone, Moon. Truly, the Moon shines
with a good grace.

[Lion *worries the mantle.*]

Theseus. Well moused, Lion.

[*Enter* Pyramus (Bottom).]

Demetrius. And then came Pyramus.

[Lion *exits.*]

255 **Lysander.** And so the lion vanished.

Bottom [*as* Pyramus]. Sweet Moon, I thank thee for thy
sunny beams.
I thank thee, Moon, for shining now so bright,
For by thy gracious, golden, glittering gleams,
I trust to take of truest Thisbe sight.—
260 But stay! O spite!
But mark, poor knight,
What dreadful dole is here!
Eyes, do you see!
How can it be!
265 O dainty duck! O dear!
Thy mantle good—
What, stained with blood?
Approach, ye Furies fell!
O Fates, come, come,
270 Cut thread and thrum,
Quail, crush, conclude, and quell!

Theseus. This passion, and the death of a dear friend,
would go near to make a man look sad.

Hippolyta. Beshrew my heart but I pity the man.

Bottom [*as* Pyramus]. O, wherefore, Nature, didst thou
lions frame,
275 Since lion vile hath here deflowered my dear,
Which is—no, no—which was the fairest dame

277 ***looked with cheer:*** wore a cheerful expression.

278 ***confound:*** destroy.

280 ***pap:*** breast.

290 ***die:*** the singular of *dice;* ***ace:*** the side of a die with one spot on it; ***but one:*** only one person, unique.

294 ***How chance:*** how does it happen that

298–301 Demetrius says that only a speck ***(mote)*** will decide which one is better—Pyramus as a man or Thisbe as a woman.

That lived, that loved, that liked, that looked with
    cheer?
Come, tears, confound!
Out, sword, and wound
280 The pap of Pyramus;
    Ay, that left pap,
    Where heart doth hop.

[Pyramus stabs himself.]

Thus die I, thus, thus, thus.
    Now am I dead;
285   Now am I fled;
My soul is in the sky.
    Tongue, lose thy light!
    Moon, take thy flight!

[Moonshine exits.]

Now die, die, die, die, die.

[Pyramus falls.]

290 **Demetrius.** No die, but an ace, for him, for he is but
    one.

Lysander. Less than an ace, man, for he is dead, he is
    nothing.

Theseus. With the help of a surgeon he might yet
    recover and yet prove an ass.

Hippolyta. How chance Moonshine is gone before
    Thisbe comes back and finds her lover?

295 **Theseus.** She will find him by starlight.

[Enter Thisbe (Flute).]

Here she comes, and her passion ends the play.

Hippolyta. Methinks she should not use a long one for
    such a Pyramus. I hope she will be brief.

Demetrius. A mote will turn the balance, which

302 *means:* moans, laments; ***videlicet:*** namely, as follows.

306 *dumb:* silent.

314 *leeks:* edible plants related to the onion.
315 ***Sisters Three:*** the Fates.

319 *shore:* shorn, cut.
320 ***his thread of silk:*** the thread of his life.

323 *imbrue:* stain with blood.

Pyramus, which Thisbe, is the better: he for a
man, God warrant us; she for a woman, God
bless us.

Lysander. She hath spied him already with those sweet
eyes.

Demetrius. And thus she means, videlicet—

Flute *[as Thisbe].*
      Asleep, my love?
      What, dead, my dove?
O Pyramus, arise!
      Speak, speak. Quite dumb?
      Dead? Dead? A tomb
Must cover thy sweet eyes.
      These lily lips,
      This cherry nose,
These yellow cowslip cheeks
      Are gone, are gone!
      Lovers, make moan;
His eyes were green as leeks.
      O Sisters Three,
      Come, come to me
With hands as pale as milk.
      Lay them in gore,
      Since you have shore
With shears his thread of silk.
      Tongue, not a word!
      Come, trusty sword,
Come, blade, my breast imbrue!

[Thisbe stabs herself.]

      And farewell, friends.
      Thus Thisbe ends.
Adieu, adieu, adieu.

[Thisbe falls.]

Theseus. Moonshine and Lion are left to bury the
dead.

331 *Bergomask dance:* a rustic dance.

333–335 Many Elizabethan plays included epilogues that asked the audience to excuse anything offensive in the performance.

338 *discharged:* performed.

340 *the iron . . . twelve:* The midnight bell has tolled 12 times.

341 *fairy time:* between midnight and dawn.

342 *outsleep:* sleep past.

343 *overwatched:* stayed up late.

344 *palpable-gross:* obviously crude.

345 *heavy gait:* slow pace.

346 *solemnity:* celebration.

350 *heavy:* tired.

351 *fordone:* exhausted.

352 *wasted brands:* burned-out logs.

354–355 *Puts . . . shroud:* makes every ill person have thoughts of death.

357–358 *the graves . . . sprite:* Every grave, wide open, lets forth its ghost.

Demetrius. Ay, and Wall too.

[Bottom and Flute arise.]

Bottom. No, I assure you, the wall is down that parted
330   their fathers. Will it please you to see the Epilogue
or to hear a Bergomask dance between two of our
company?

Theseus. No epilogue, I pray you. For your play needs
no excuse. Never excuse. For when the players are
335   all dead, there need none to be blamed. Marry, if he
that writ it had played Pyramus and hanged himself
in Thisbe's garter, it would have been a fine tragedy;
and so it is, truly, and very notably discharged. But,
come, your Bergomask. Let your epilogue alone.

[Dance, and the players exit.]

340   The iron tongue of midnight hath told twelve.
Lovers, to bed! 'Tis almost fairy time.
I fear we shall outsleep the coming morn
As much as we this night have overwatched.
This palpable-gross play hath well beguiled
345   The heavy gait of night. Sweet friends, to bed.
A fortnight hold we this solemnity
In nightly revels and new jollity.

[They exit.]

[Enter Robin Goodfellow.]

Robin. Now the hungry lion roars,
    And the wolf behowls the moon,
350   Whilst the heavy plowman snores,
    All with weary task fordone.
Now the wasted brands do glow,
    Whilst the screech-owl, screeching loud,
Puts the wretch that lies in woe
355   In remembrance of a shroud.
Now it is the time of night
    That the graves, all gaping wide,

361 *triple Hecate:* a goddess of the moon, earth, and underworld who became associated with witchcraft and sorcery.

364 *frolic:* frolicsome, merry.

382 *the issue there create:* the offspring created there.

386 *blots:* deformities.

389 *mark prodigious:* ominous birthmark.

Every one lets forth his sprite
    In the church-way paths to glide.
360 And we fairies, that do run
    By the triple Hecate's team
From the presence of the sun,
    Following darkness like a dream,
Now are frolic. Not a mouse
365 Shall disturb this hallowed house.
I am sent with broom before,
To sweep the dust behind the door.

[Enter Oberon and Titania, King and Queen of Fairies, with all their train.]

Oberon. Through the house give glimmering light,
    By the dead and drowsy fire.
370 Every elf and fairy sprite,
    Hop as light as bird from brier,
And this ditty after me,
Sing and dance it trippingly.

Titania. First rehearse your song by rote,
375 To each word a warbling note.
Hand in hand, with fairy grace,
Will we sing and bless this place.

[Oberon leads the Fairies in song and dance.]

Oberon. Now, until the break of day,
    Through this house each fairy stray.
380 To the best bride-bed will we,
Which by us shall blessèd be,
And the issue there create
Ever shall be fortunate.
So shall all the couples three
385 Ever true in loving be,
And the blots of Nature's hand
Shall not in their issue stand.
Never mole, harelip, nor scar,
    Nor mark prodigious, such as are
390 Despisèd in nativity,

392 *field-dew consecrate:* consecrated dew (the fairies' holy water).

393 *take his gait:* go his way.

394 *several:* separate.

404 *idle:* foolish.

405 *No more . . . dream:* producing no more than a dream.

407 *mend:* improve.

409–410 *If we . . . tongue:* if we are lucky enough to escape hissing from the audience.

414 *Give me your hands:* applaud.

415 *restore amends:* make amends, repay your kindness.

Shall upon their children be.
With this field-dew consecrate
Every fairy take his gait,
And each several chamber bless,
395   Through this palace, with sweet peace.
And the owner of it blest,
Ever shall in safety rest.
Trip away. Make no stay.
Meet me all by break of day.

[All but Robin *exit.]*

400   **Robin.** If we shadows have offended,
Think but this and all is mended:
That you have but slumbered here
While these visions did appear.
And this weak and idle theme,
405   No more yielding but a dream,
Gentles, do not reprehend.
If you pardon, we will mend.
And, as I am an honest Puck,
If we have unearnèd luck
410   Now to 'scape the serpent's tongue,
We will make amends ere long.
Else the Puck a liar call.
So good night unto you all.
Give me your hands, if we be friends,
415   And Robin shall restore amends.

[He exits.]

Related Readings

CONTENTS

A Midsummer Night's Dream

by Norrie Epstein

At first glance, Shakespeare's comedy may seem like nothing more than a pleasant, dreamlike fairy tale. In the following essay, Norrie Epstein offers a more probing analysis of the play, showing how it "reveals . . . deep truths about our hidden emotional life."

Like a dream itself, *A Midsummer Night's Dream* presents a startling mixture of disparate elements: homely and realistic characters are placed within a fantastic, almost surrealistic, plot; the lowest level of society mixes with the highest; prosaic speech is uttered along with sublime poetry; and the supernatural, the human, and the bestial worlds commingle. And, like a dream, this dramatic fairy tale initially appears to be a trivial diversion that bears little connection to our waking lives. Yet, upon closer examination, *A Midsummer Night's Dream* reveals, in disguised form, deep truths about our hidden emotional life.

In *A Midsummer Night's Dream* Shakespeare does something with his two central pairs of lovers that he had never done before and would do only once again (with Rosencrantz and Guildenstern in *Hamlet*): he creates characters who are interchangeable—a striking departure for a playwright who usually distinguishes every character, no matter how minor. Lysander loves Hermia, and Hermia, Lysander;

169

Demetrius also loves Hermia; and Helena, odd woman out, is infatuated with Demetrius. But any combination would serve the purposes of the plot. No matter how many times you read this play, you'll get Hermia and Helena confused. The only difference between them is that one is tall, the other short; they are the stock lovers found in any romantic comedy— except that, this being Shakespeare, they speak more beautifully. The same is true of the men: Lysander could suddenly become Demetrius and the audience would never be any the wiser. That's precisely Shakespeare's point; this play, which deals in magic, illusion, and enchantment, is about the mysterious power of love to transform an ordinary mortal into a rarity of perfection:

> Things base and vile, holding no quantity,
> Love can transpose to form and dignity.
> Love looks not with the eyes, but with the mind . . .

> (I.1.232–34)

But since we aren't under the lovers' spell, we see them with the cool eyes of reason, and they all look alike to us. And apparently to Puck as well. When Oberon orders him to sprinkle "love juice" in the eyes of an Athenian man, he mistakes Lysander for Demetrius, the intended recipient. Thus Lysander, once passionate about Hermia, is now deeply in love with Helena. Then, to rectify his error, Puck squeezes the juice onto Demetrius, and he, too, falls for the once-despised Helena. Love, long recognized as a form of enchantment, literally becomes a spell.

Modern audiences tend to resist the idea of magic, but many Elizabethans still believed in fairies, only their creatures were much darker and more sinister than the bland images manufactured by Walt Disney.

Their traditional habitat, the dark forest where confused travelers lose their way, belongs more to the strange tales of the Brothers Grimm. Shakespeare's moon-drenched fairy world is a symbolic dreamscape where traditional distinctions blur and disappear. By entering the enchanted woods at nightfall, the lovers abandon the familiar daylight world, as represented by civilized Athens, and enter a mental landscape, a covert realm within the unconscious, a place of fearsome transformations and self-discovery. Just as insanity, poetry, and dreams possess their own fantastic logic, revealing an unsettling yet truthful vision of ordinary life, so the dark woodlands—as seen in countless myths and fairy tales—expose the flip side of civilization, revealing the tenuous boundary that distinguishes reason and madness, lust and love.

Although the characters have transferred their affections, the situation remains the same: Hermia is merely exchanged for Helena. If the play were translated into modern life, Lysander, Hermia, Demetrius, and Helena would be Bob and Carol and Ted and Alice.

Meanwhile, there are other visitors to the forest that night. The Athenian tradesmen have gathered there to rehearse the "tedious brief scene of young Pyramus and Thisbe," which they intend to perform for Duke Theseus in honor of his forthcoming nuptials. As he watches them rehearse, Puck snickers at their amateurish bungling, just as he mocks the inanity of the young lovers: "Shall we their fond pageants see? / Lord, what fools these mortals be!" ("Fond" meant foolish.) From Puck's superior perspective, the mortal world is a ridiculous farce, and he laughs at the confused lovers just as later the lovers will snicker at the artisans when they put on *their* show. If in *Lear* human beings are to the gods as flies are to wanton boys, in *Dream* they are sport for fairies.

But the fairy kingdom is not immune to disorder. In Oberon and Titania's bitter feud, the theme of love's delusion is carried to an even darker extreme. Enraged at Titania's refusal to give him her beloved Indian boy, Oberon sprinkles the love juice in Titania's eyes while hissing this malediction:

What thou seest when thou dost wake,
Do it for thy true love take;
Love and languish for his sake.
Be it ounce or cat or bear,
Pard, or boar with bristled hair
In thy eye that shall appear
When thou wakest, it is thy dear.
Wake when some vile thing is near!

(II.2.33–40)

Unfortunately, it's the newly "translated" Bottom who, thanks to Puck's mischief, is now crowned with the head of an ass. Titania, that most ethereal queen, is immediately enamored of the animal that was regarded as the most lascivious—and sexually potent—in the Elizabethan bestiary. Only in this century have critics paid much attention to the grotesquely erotic implications of Titania and Bottom's love scene:

Come, sit thee down upon this flowery bed
  While I thy amiable cheeks do coy,*
And stick muskroses in thy sleek, smooth head,
  And kiss thy fair large ears, my gentle joy.

(IV.1.1–4)

*Coy means "caress."

In *A Midsummer Night's Dream* the question, "What does she (or he) see in him (c is taken to an extreme: Who among us, Shal seems to ask, hasn't fallen for an ass and believeu nim (or her) a god?

And who, upon awakening from the enchantment of love, has not been embarrassed to discover the mistake?

Released from her spell, Titania shudders, half remembering, not quite certain of what she has done, or if what has happened is real or an illusion. Similarly, the lovers, their confusion dispelled by Puck and Oberon, fall into a deep sleep and wake never knowing if their experiences have been a vision or reality. Perhaps a little of both. As Hermia says: "Methinks I see these things with parted eye, / When everything seems double." Exhausted by their ordeal, they all "to Athens back again repair / And think no more of this night's accidents / But as the fierce vexation of a dream." Demetrius still retains the effects of the love potion, leaving us to wonder if his love for Helena is "real"; but as Shakespeare has already shown us, all love—even "true" love—is a form of sorcery. And, after all, this is a comedy, and everyone must get married.

All the different plots and social strata come together in the final scene, when the artisans assemble before lovers and nobles to put on their play in honor of the weddings. Scholars believe that *A Midsummer Night's Dream* was written to grace the marriage of a noble couple, so in essence, Shakespeare's original audience watched a play that contained a play that was watched by courtiers. The levels of deception and mirror images in this play are astonishing, and it's easy to get trapped amid all the shimmering reflections. Ironically, it's the oafish Bottom who has the wisest comment on the night's experiences, and students and scholars of Shakespeare would do well to pay attention:

> I have had a most rare vision. I have had a dream past the wit of man to say what dream it was. Man is but an ass if he go about to expound this dream.
>
> (IV.1.203–5)

The Song of Wandering Aengus

by William Butler Yeats

*For centuries, poets have followed
Shakespeare's footsteps into the magical
woods. In this 20th-century poem, the
speaker recalls the time he went fishing
and beheld an astounding transformation,
which haunts his life still.*

I went out to the hazel wood,
Because a fire was in my head,
And cut and peeled a hazel wand,
And hooked a berry to a thread;
5 And when white moths were on the wing,
And moth-like stars were flickering out,
I dropped the berry in a stream
And caught a little silver trout.

When I had laid it on the floor
10 I went to blow the fire aflame,
But something rustled on the floor,
And some one called me by my name:
It had become a glimmering girl
With apple blossom in her hair
15 Who called me by my name and ran
And faded through the brightening air.

Though I am old with wandering
Through hollow lands and hilly lands,
I will find out where she has gone,

20   And kiss her lips and take her hands;
    And walk among long dappled grass,
    And pluck till time and times are done
    The silver apples of the moon,
    The golden apples of the sun.

The Sweet Miracle / El Dulce Milagro

by Juana de Ibarbourou
translated by Alice Stone Blackwell

In Shakespeare's play, love was associated with transformative powers. Bottom the Weaver took on the head of an ass and became Titania's beloved, thanks to Robin Goodfellow's magic and his love nectar. In one way or another, each of the lovers in the play is transformed by the experience of love. This poem describes another kind of miraculous transformation brought about my love.

Oh, what is this? A miracle! My hands are
    blossoming!
See, roses, roses, roses forth from my fingers
    spring.
My lover kissed my hands, and then a charm
    wrought silently;
Upon them flowers came softly out, as stars
    do in the sky.

5   And now the people murmur, who behold
    me as I roam:
"Don't you see that she is crazy? Poor
    woman! Send her home.
She says that roses from her hands are born
    in wondrous wise,
And as she goes she waves them, like flitting
    butterflies."

Ah, foolish, foolish people, with minds too
    dull and slow
10 To grasp a marvel such as this! Alas they
    only know
That nowhere save on rosebushes are born
    red roses sweet,
And only in the wheat-fields men gather ears
    of wheat.

But let them call me crazy, and shut me in a
    cell,
And lock the door with seven keys, to close it
    fast and well;
15 And let them set a watch-dog beside the
    portal, too,
A warder rough and savage, a warder tried
    and true.

I still shall sing the same thing: "My hands
    are blossoming!
Sweet roses, roses, roses out of my fingers
    spring!"
And wondrous fragrance through my cell will
    breathe by night and day,
20 As if 'twere filled with roses fair of France, a
    vast bouquet!

El Dulce Milagro

by Juana de Ibarbourou

Que es esto? ¡Prodigio! Mis manos florecen;
rosas, rosas, rosas a mis dedos crecen.
Mi amante besóme las manos, y en ellas
¡oh, gracia! brotaron rosas como estrellas.

5   Y murmura al verme la gente que pasa:
—¿No veis que está loca? Tornadla a su casa.
¡Dice que en las manos le han nacido rosas
y las va agitando como mariposas!

¡Ah, la gente necia que nunca comprende
10   un milagro de éstos, y que sólo entiende
que no nacen rosas más que en los rosales
y que no hay más trigo que el de los trigales!

Que me digan loca, que en celda me encierren;
que con siete llaves la puerta me cierren;
15   que junto a la puerta pongan un lebrel,
carcelero rudo, carcelero fiel.

Cantaré lo mismo;—Mis manos florecen,
rosas, rosas, rosas a mis dedos crecen. . .
¡Y toda mi celda tendrá la fragrancia
20   de un inmenso ramo de rosas de Francia!

April Witch

by Ray Bradbury

*Like Robin Goodfellow in Shakespeare's
play, young Cecy possesses magical
powers: she "can live in anything at all—a
pebble, a crocus, or a praying mantis." On
this starry spring night, when all of nature
seems bursting with romance, Cecy
decides to experience love first hand. To
realize her dream, she needs the
cooperation of a farm girl and her would-
be boyfriend.*

Into the air, over the valleys, under the stars, above
a river, a pond, a road, flew Cecy. Invisible as new
spring winds, fresh as the breath of clover rising from
twilight fields, she flew. She soared in doves as soft as
white ermine, stopped in trees and lived in blossoms,
showering away in petals when the breeze blew. She
perched in a lime-green frog, cool as mint by a shining
pool. She trotted in a brambly dog and barked to hear
echoes from the sides of distant barns. She lived in new
April grasses, in sweet clear liquids rising from the
musky earth.

It's spring, thought Cecy. I'll be in every living thing
in the world to-night.

Now she inhabited neat crickets on the tar-pool
roads, now prickled in dew on an iron gate. Hers was
an adaptably quick mind flowing unseen upon Illinois
winds on this one evening of her life when she was just
seventeen.

"I want to be in love," she said.

She had said it at supper. And her parents had
widened their eyes and stiffened back in their chairs.

"Patience," had been their advice. "Remember, you're remarkable. Our whole family is odd and remarkable. We can't mix or marry with ordinary folk. We'd lose our magical powers if we did. You wouldn't want to lose your ability to 'travel' by magic, would you? Then be careful. Be careful!"

But in her high bedroom, Cecy had touched perfume to her throat and stretched out, trembling and apprehensive, on her four-poster, as a moon the colour of milk rose over Illinois country, turning rivers to cream and roads to platinum.

"Yes," she sighed. "I'm one of an odd family. We sleep days and fly nights like black kites on the wind. If we want, we can sleep in moles through the winter, in the warm earth. I can live in anything at all—a pebble, a crocus, or a praying mantis. I can leave my plain, bony body behind and send my mind far out for adventure. Now!"

The wind whipped her away over fields and meadows.

She saw the warm spring lights of cottages and farms glowing with twilight colours.

If I can't be in love, myself, because I'm plain and odd, then I'll be in love through someone else, she thought.

Outside a farmhouse in the spring night a dark-haired girl, no more than nineteen, drew up water from a deep stone well. She was singing.

Cecy fell—a green leaf—into the well. She lay in the tender moss of the well, gazing up through dark coolness. Now she quickened in a fluttering, invisible amoeba. Now in a water droplet! At last, within a cold cup, she felt herself lifted to the girl's warm lips. There was a soft night sound of drinking.

Cecy looked out from the girl's eyes.

She entered into the dark head and gazed from the shining eyes at the hands pulling the rough rope. She listened through the shell ears to this girl's world. She smelled a particular universe through these delicate nostrils, felt this special heart beating, beating. Felt this strange tongue move with singing.

Does she know I'm here? thought Cecy.

The girl gasped. She stared into the night meadows. "Who's there?"

No answer.

"Only the wind," whispered Cecy.

"Only the wind." The girl laughed at herself, but shivered.

It was a good body, this girl's body. It held bones of finest slender ivory hidden and roundly fleshed. This brain was like a pink tea rose, hung in darkness, and there was cider-wine in this mouth. The lips lay firm on the white, white teeth and the brows arched neatly at the world, and the hair blew soft and fine on her milky neck. The pores knit small and close. The nose tilted at the moon and the cheeks glowed like small fires. The body drifted with feather-balances from one motion to another and seemed always singing to itself. Being in this body, this head, was like basking in a hearth fire, living in the purr of a sleeping cat, stirring in warm creek waters that flowed by night to the sea.

I'll like it here, thought Cecy.

"What?" asked the girl, as if she'd heard a voice.

"What's your name," asked Cecy carefully.

"Ann Leary." The girl twitched. "Now why should I say *that* out loud?"

"Ann, Ann," whispered Cecy. "Ann, you're going to be in love."

As if to answer this, a great roar sprang from the road, a clatter and a ring of wheels on gravel. A tall man drove up in a rig, holding the reins high with his monstrous arms, his smile glowing across the yard.

"Ann!"

"Is that you, Tom?"

"Who else?" Leaping from the rig, he tied the reins to the fence.

"I'm not speaking to you!" Ann whirled, the bucket in her hands slopping.

"No!" cried Cecy.

Ann froze. She looked at the hills and the first spring stars. She stared at the man named Tom. Cecy made her drop the bucket.

"Look what you've done!"

Tom ran up.

"Look what you *made* me do!"

He wiped her shoes with a handkerchief, laughing.

"Get away!" She kicked at his hands, but he laughed again, and gazing down on him from miles away, Cecy saw the turn of his head, the size of his skull, the flare of his nose, the shine of his eye, the girth of his shoulder, and the hard strength of his hands doing this delicate thing with the handkerchief. Peering down from the secret attic of this lovely head, Cecy yanked a hidden copper ventriloquist's wire and the pretty mouth popped wide: "Thank you!"

"Oh, so you *have* manners?" The smell of leather on his hands, the smell of the horse rose from his clothes into the tender nostrils, and Cecy, far, far away over night meadows and flowered fields, stirred as with some dream in her bed.

"Not for you, no!" said Ann.

"Hush, speak gently," said Cecy. She moved Ann's fingers out toward Tom's head. Ann snatched them back.

"I've gone mad!"

"You have." He nodded, smiling but bewildered. "Were you going to touch me then?"

"I don't know. Oh, go away!" Her cheeks glowed with pink charcoals.

"Why don't you run? I'm not stopping you." Tom got up. "Have you changed your mind? Will you go to the dance with me to-night? It's special. Tell you why later."

"No," said Ann.

"Yes!" cried Cecy. "I've never danced. I want to dance. I've never worn a long gown, all rustly. I want that. I want to dance all night. I've never known what it's like to be in a woman, dancing; Father and Mother would never permit it. Dogs, cats, locusts, leaves, everything else in the world at one time or another I've known, but never a woman in the spring, never on a night like this. Oh, please—we *must* go to that dance!"

She spread her thought like the fingers of a hand within a new glove.

"Yes," said Ann Leary, "I'll go. I don't know why, but I'll go to the dance with you to-night, Tom."

"Now inside, quick!" cried Cecy. "You must wash, tell your folks, get your gown ready, out with the iron, into your room!"

"Mother," said Ann, "I've changed my mind!"

The rig was galloping off down the pike, the rooms of the farmhouse jumped to life, water was boiling for a bath, the coal stove was heating an iron to press the gown, the mother was rushing about with a fringe of hair pins in her mouth. "What's come over you, Ann? You don't like Tom!"

"That's true." Ann stopped amidst the great fever.

But it's spring! thought Cecy.

"It's spring," said Ann.

And it's a fine night for dancing, thought Cecy.

". . . for dancing," murmured Ann Leary.

Then she was in the tub and the soap creaming on her white seal shoulders, small nests of soap beneath her arms, and the flesh of her warm breasts moving in her hands and Cecy moving the mouth, making the smile, keeping the actions going. There must be no pause, no hesitation, or the entire pantomime might fall in ruins! Ann Leary must be kept moving, doing, acting, wash here, soap there, now out! Rub with a towel! Now perfume and powder!

"You!" Ann caught herself in the mirror, all whiteness and pinkness like lilies and carnations. "*Who* are you to-night?"

"I'm a girl seventeen." Cecy gazed from her violet eyes. "You can't see me. Do you know I'm here?"

Ann Leary shook her head. "I've rented my body to an April witch, for sure."

"*Close*, very close!" laughed Cecy. "Now, on with your dressing."

The luxury of feeling good clothes move over an ample body! And then the halloo outside.

"Ann, Tom's back!"

"Tell him to wait." Ann sat down suddenly. "Tell him I'm not going to that dance."

"What?" said her mother, in the door.

Cecy snapped back into attention. It had been a fatal relaxing, a fatal moment of leaving Ann's body for only an instant. She had heard the distant sound of horses' hoofs and the rig rambling through moonlit spring country. For a second she thought, I'll go find Tom and sit in his head and see what it's like to be in a man of twenty-two on a night like this. And so she had started quickly across a heather field, but now, like a bird to a cage, flew back and rustled and beat about in Ann Leary's head.

"Ann!"

"Tell him to go away!"

"Ann!" Cecy settled down and spread her thoughts.

But Ann had the bit in her mouth now. "No, no, I hate him!"

I shouldn't have left—even for a moment. Cecy poured her mind into the hands of the young girl, into the heart, into the head, softly, softly. *Stand up*, she thought.

Ann stood.

Put on your coat!

Ann put on her coat.

Now, march!

No! thought Ann Leary.

March!

"Ann," said her mother, "don't keep Tom waiting another minute. You get on out there now and no nonsense. What's come over you?"

"Nothing, Mother. Good night. We'll be home late."

Ann and Cecy ran together into the spring evening.

A room full of softly dancing pigeons ruffling their quiet, trailing feathers, a room full of peacocks, a room full of rainbow eyes and lights. And in the centre of it, around, around, around, danced Ann Leary.

"Oh, it *is* a fine evening," said Cecy.

"Oh, it's a fine evening," said Ann.

"You're odd," said Tom.

The music whirled them in dimness, in rivers of song; they floated, they bobbed, they sank down, they arose for air, they gasped, they clutched each other like drowning people and whirled on again, in fan motions, in whispers and sighs, to "Beautiful Ohio."

Cecy hummed. Ann's lips parted and the music came out.

"Yes, I'm odd," said Cecy.

"You're not the same," said Tom.

"No, not to-night."

"You're not the Ann Leary I knew."

"No, not at all, at all," whispered Cecy, miles and miles away. "No, not at all," said the moved lips.

"I've the funniest feeling," said Tom.

"About what?"

"About you." He held her back and danced her and looked into her glowing face, watching for something.

"Your eyes," he said, "I can't figure it."

"Do you see *me*?" asked Cecy.

"Part of you's here, Ann, and part of you's not." Tom turned her carefully, his face uneasy.

"Yes."

"Why did you come with me?"

"I didn't want to come," said Ann.

"Why, then?"

"Something made me."

"What?"

"I don't know." Ann's voice was faintly hysterical.

"Now, now, hush, hush," whispered Cecy. "Hush, that's it. Around, around."

They whispered and rustled and rose and fell away in the dark room, with the music moving and turning them.

"But you *did* come to the dance," said Tom.

"I did," said Cecy.

"Here." And he danced her lightly out an open door and walked her quietly away from the hall and the music and the people.

They climbed up and sat together in the rig.

"Ann," he said, taking her hands, trembling. "Ann." But the way he said her name it was as if it wasn't her name. He kept glancing into her pale face, and now her eyes were open again. "I used to love you, you know that," he said.

"I know."

"But you've always been fickle and I didn't want to be hurt."

"It's just as well, we're very young," said Ann.

"No, I mean to say, I'm sorry," said Cecy.

"What *do* you mean?" Tom dropped her hands and stiffened.

The night was warm and the smell of the earth shimmered up all about them where they sat, and the fresh trees breathed one leaf against another in a shaking and rustling.

"I don't know," said Ann.

"Oh, but *I* know," said Cecy. "You're tall and you're the finest-looking man in all the world. This is a good evening; this is an evening I'll always remember, being with you." She put out the alien cold hand to find his reluctant hand again and bring it back, and warm it and hold it very tight.

"But," said Tom, blinking, "to-night you're here, you're there. One minute one way, the next minute another. I wanted to take you to the dance tonight for old times' sake. I meant nothing by it when I first asked you. And then, when we were standing at the well, I knew something had changed, really changed, about you. You were different. There was something new and soft, something . . ." He groped for a word. "I don't know, I can't say. The way you looked. Something about your voice. And I know I'm in love with you again."

"No," said Cecy. "With me, with *me*."

"And I'm afraid of being in love with you," he said. "You'll hurt me again."

"I might," said Ann.

No, no, I'd love you with all my heart! thought Cecy. Ann, say it to him, say it for me. Say you'd love him with all your heart.

Ann said nothing.

Tom moved quietly closer and put his hand up to hold her chin. "I'm going away. I've got a job a hundred miles from here. Will you miss me?"

"Yes," said Ann and Cecy.

"May I kiss you good-bye, then?"

"Yes," said Cecy before anyone else could speak.

He placed his lips to the strange mouth. He kissed the strange mouth and he was trembling.

Ann sat like a white statue.

"Ann!" said Cecy. "Move your arms, hold him!"

She sat like a carved wooden doll in the moonlight. Again he kissed her lips.

"I do love you," whispered Cecy. "I'm here, it's me you saw in her eyes, it's me, and I love you if she never will."

He moved away and seemed like a man who had run a long distance. He sat beside her. "I don't know what's happening. For a moment there . . ."

"Yes?" asked Cecy.

"For a moment I thought—" He put his hands to his eyes. "Never mind. Shall I take you home now?"

"Please," said Ann Leary.

He clucked to the horse, snapped the reins tiredly, and drove the rig away. They rode in the rustle and slap and motion of the moonlit rig in the still early, only eleven o'clock spring night, with the shining meadows and sweet fields of clover gliding by.

And Cecy, looking at the fields and meadows, thought, It would be worth it, it would be worth everything to be with him from this night on. And she heard her parents' voices again, faintly, "Be careful. You wouldn't want to lose your magical powers, would you—married to a mere mortal? Be careful. You wouldn't want that."

Yes, yes, thought Cecy, even that I'd give up, here and now, if he would have me. I wouldn't need to roam the spring nights then, I wouldn't need to live in birds and dogs and cats and foxes, I'd need only be with him. Only him. Only him.

The road passed under, whispering.

"Tom," said Ann at last.

"What?" He stared coldly at the road, the horse, the trees, the sky, the stars.

"If you're ever, in years to come, at any time, in Green Town, Illinois, a few miles from here, will you do me a favour?"

"Perhaps."

"Will you do me the favour of stopping and seeing a friend of mine?" Ann Leary said this haltingly, awkwardly.

"Why?"

"She's a good friend. I've told her of you. I'll give you her address. Just a moment." When the rig stopped at her farm she drew forth a pencil and paper from her small purse and wrote in the moonlight, pressing the paper to her knee. "There it is. Can you read it?"

He glanced at the paper and nodded bewilderedly.

"Cecy Elliott, 12 Willow Street, Green Town, Illinois," he said.

"Will you visit her someday?" asked Ann.

"Someday," he said.

"Promise?"

"What has this to do with us?" he cried savagely. "What do I want with names and papers?" He crumpled the paper into a tight ball and shoved it in his coat.

"Oh, please promise!" begged Cecy.

". . . promise . . ." said Ann.

"All right, all right, now let me be!" he shouted.

I'm tired, thought Cecy. I can't stay. I have to go home. I'm weakening. I've only the power to stay a few hours out like this in the night, travelling, travelling. But before I go . . .

". . . before I go," said Ann.

She kissed Tom on the lips.

"This is me kissing you," said Cecy.

Tom held her off and looked at Ann Leary and looked deep, deep inside. He said nothing, but his face began to relax slowly, very slowly, and the lines vanished away, and his mouth softened from its hardness, and he looked deep again into the moonlit face held here before him.

Then he put her off the rig and without so much as

good night was driving swiftly down the road.

Cecy let go.

Ann Leary, crying out, released from prison, it seemed, raced up the moonlit path to her house and slammed the door.

Cecy lingered for only a little while. In the eyes of a cricket she saw the spring night world. In the eyes of a frog she sat for a lonely moment by a pool. In the eyes of a night bird she looked down from a tall, moon-haunted elm and saw the lights go out in two farmhouses, one here, one a mile away. She thought of herself and her family, and her strange power, and the fact that no one in the family could ever marry any one of the people in this vast world out here beyond the hills.

"Tom?" Her weakening mind flew in a night bird under the trees and over deep fields of wild mustard. "Have you still got the paper, Tom? Will you come by someday, some year, sometime, to see me? Will you know me then? Will you look in my face and remember then where it was you saw me last and know that you love me as I love you, with all my heart for all time?"

She paused in the cool night air, a million miles from towns and people, above farms and continents and rivers and hills. "Tom?" softly.

Tom was asleep. It was deep night; his clothes were hung on chairs or folded neatly over the end of the bed. And in one silent, carefully unflung hand upon the white pillow, by his head, was a small piece of paper with writing on it. Slowly, slowly, a fraction of an inch at a time, his fingers closed down upon and held it tightly. And he did not even stir or notice when a blackbird, faintly, wondrously, beat softly for a moment against the clear moon crystals of the windowpane, then, fluttering quietly, stopped and flew away toward the east, over the sleeping earth.

Come. And Be My Baby

by Maya Angelou

Shakespeare's lovers in A Midsummer Night's Dream *sought refuge in the woods, where they could be free from the restrictions of Athens. In this poem the speaker looks to love as an escape from the dilemmas and turmoil of life in the modern world.*

The highway is full of big cars
going nowhere fast
And folks is smoking anything that'll burn
Some people wrap their lives around a
    cocktail glass
5 And you sit wondering
where you're going to turn
I got it.
Come. And be my baby.

Some prophets say the world is gonna end
    tomorrow
10 But others say we've got a week or two
The paper is full of every kind of blooming
    horror
And you sit wondering
What you're gonna do.
I got it.
15 Come. And be my baby.

Love's Initiations

from Care of the Soul

by Thomas Moore

As the lovers discovered in A Midsummer Night's Dream, *love can lead us from the depths of agony to the heights of ecstasy, often for reasons that we cannot begin to understand. Thomas Moore, a well-known psychologist, analyzes love "as a kind of madness" and seeks to explain what we can learn from its power.*

Love is a kind of madness, Plato said, a divine madness. Today we talk about love as though it were primarily an aspect of relationship and also, to a great degree, as if it were something within our control. We're concerned about how to do it right, how to make it successful, how to overcome its problems, and how to survive its failures. Many of the problems people bring to therapy involve the high expectations and the rock-bottom experiences of love. It is clear that love is never simple, that it brings with it struggles of the past and hopes for the future, and that it is loaded with material that may be remotely—if at all—connected to the person who is the apparent object of love.

We sometimes talk about love lightly, not acknowledging how powerful and lasting it can be. We always expect love to be healing and whole, and then are astonished to find that it can create hollow gaps and empty failures. Going through a divorce is often a long and painful process that never truly ends. Often we never know completely if we've done the right thing, and even if we enjoy some peace of mind about the decision, memory and attachment continue to persist, if only in dreams. People are also tortured emotionally about love that was never expressed. A woman cries whenever she thinks of her father going into surgery the last time she saw him. She felt a strong urge within herself to tell him that she loved him, even though their relationship had been strained all her life, but she held back, and then it was too late. Her remorse is bitter and persistent. In his *Symposium*, his great book on the nature of love, Plato called love the child of fullness and emptiness. Each of these aspects somehow accompanies the other.

Our love of love and our high expectations that it will somehow make life complete seem to be an integral part of the experience. Love seems to promise that life's gaping wounds will close up and heal. It makes little difference that in the past love has shown itself to be painful and disturbing. There is something self-renewing in love. Like the goddesses of Greece, it is able to renew its virginity in a bath of forgetfulness.

I suppose we do learn some things about love each time we experience it. In the failure of a relationship we resolve never to make the same mistakes again. We get toughened to some extent and perhaps become a little wiser. But love itself is eternally young and always manifests some of the folly of youth. So, maybe it is better not to become too jaded by love's suffering and dead ends, but rather to appreciate that emptiness is part of love's heritage and therefore its very nature. It isn't necessary to make strong efforts to avoid past mistakes or to learn how to be clever about love. The advance we make after we have been devastated by love may be to be able simply to enter it freely once again, in spite of our suspicions, to draw ever closer to the darkness and hollowness that are mysteriously necessary in love.

It may be useful to consider love less as an aspect of relationship and more as an event of the soul. This is the point of view taken in ancient handbooks. There is no talk about making relationships work, although there is celebration of friendship and intimacy. The emphasis is on what love does to the soul. Does it bring broader vision? Does it initiate the soul in some way? Does it carry the lover away from earth to an awareness of divine things?

Ficino says, "What is human love? What is its purpose? It is the desire for union with a beautiful object in order to make eternity available to mortal life." It is a fundamental teaching of the Neo-platonists that earthly pleasures are an invitation to eternal delights. Ficino says that these things of ordinary life that enchant us toward eternity are "magical decoys." In other words, what appears to be a fully earthly relationship between two human individuals is at the same time a path toward far deeper experiences of the soul. Love confuses its victims because its work in the soul does not always coincide in every detail with the apparent tempos and requirements of relationship. The early Romantic German poet Novalis put it quite simply: love, he says, was not made for this world.

Freud offers one way of turning our focus in love away from the contingencies of life and toward the soul. He says that love always involves a transference to the present relationship of early family patterns. Father, mother, brother, and sister are always implicated in love as invisible but influential presences. Freud turns our attention toward deeper fantasies that wake into action when love stirs. Of course, we can read Freud reductionistically as saying that the present love is only an old love resurrected.

Or we can be invited by Freud to consider how love makes the soul fertile with memories and images. . . .

A general principle we can take from Freud is that love sparks imagination into extraordinary activity. Being "in love" is like being "in imagination." The literal concerns of everyday life, yesterday such a preoccupation, now practically disappear in the rush of love's daydreams. Concrete reality recedes as the imaginal world settles in. Thus, the "divine madness" of love is akin to the mania of paranoia and other dissociations.

Does this mean that we need to be cured of this madness? Robert Burton in his massive self-help book of the seventeenth century, *The Anatomy of Melancholy*, says there is only one cure for the melancholic sickness of love: enter into it with abandon. Some authors today argue that romantic love is such an illusion that we need to distrust it and keep our wits about us so that we are not led astray. But warnings like this betray a distrust of the soul. We may need to be cured by love of our attachment to life without fantasy. Maybe one function of love is to cure us of an anemic imagination, a life emptied of romantic attachment and abandoned to reason.

Love releases us into the realm of divine imagination, where the soul is expanded and reminded of its unearthly cravings and needs. We think that when a lover inflates his loved one he is failing to acknowledge her flaws—"Love is blind." But it may be the other way around. Love allows a person to see the true angelic nature of another person, the halo, the aureole of divinity. Certainly from the perspective of ordinary life this is madness and illusion. But if we let loose our hold on our philosophies and psychologies of enlightenment and reason, we might learn to appreciate the perspective of eternity that enters life as madness, Plato's divine frenzy.

The Sensible Thing

by F. Scott Fitzgerald

In Shakespeare's play, the young lovers leave the familiar world behind to pursue their love interests. In similar fashion, the main character in this story, George O'Kelley, suddenly abandons his job in New York City to win back his beloved Jonquil in Tennessee. George and Jonquil must decide between their romantic dreams and doing "the sensible thing."

At the Great American Lunch Hour young George O'Kelly straightened his desk deliberately and with an assumed air of interest. No one in the office must know that he was in a hurry, for success is a matter of atmosphere, and it is not well to advertise the fact that your mind is separated from your work by a distance of seven hundred miles.

But once out of the building he set his teeth and began to run, glancing now and then at the gay noon of early spring which filled Times Square and loitered less than twenty feet over the heads of the crowd. The crowd all looked slightly upward and took deep March breaths, and the sun dazzled their eyes so that scarcely any one saw any one else but only their own reflection on the sky.

George O'Kelly, whose mind was over seven hundred miles away, thought that all outdoors was horrible. He rushed into the subway, and for ninety-five blocks bent a frenzied glance on a car-card which showed vividly how he had only one chance in five of keeping his teeth for ten years. At 137th Street he broke off his study of commercial art, left the subway, and began to run again, a tireless, anxious run that brought him this time to his home—one room in a high, horrible apartment house in the middle of nowhere.

There it was on the bureau, the letter—in sacred ink, on blessed paper—all over the city, people, if they listened, could hear the beating of George O'Kelly's heart. He read the commas, the blots, and the thumb-smudge on the margin—then he threw himself hopelessly upon his bed.

He was in a mess, one of those terrific messes which are ordinary incidents in the life of the poor, which follow poverty like birds of prey. The poor go under or go up or go wrong or even go on, somehow, in a way the poor have—but George O'Kelly was so new to poverty that had any one denied the uniqueness of his case he would have been astounded.

Less than two years ago he had been graduated with honors from The Massachusetts Institute of Technology and had taken a position with a firm of construction engineers in southern Tennessee. All his life he had thought in terms of tunnels and skyscrapers and great squat dams and tall, three-towered bridges, that were like dancers holding hands in a row, with heads as tall as cities and skirts of cable strand. It had seemed romantic to George O'Kelly to change the sweep of rivers and the shape of mountains so that life could flourish in the old bad lands of the world where it had never taken root before. He loved steel, and there was always steel near him in his dreams, liquid steel, steel in bars, and blocks and beams and formless plastic masses, waiting for him, as paint and canvas to his hand. Steel inexhaustible, to be made lovely and austere in his imaginative fire . . .

At present he was an insurance clerk at forty dollars a week with his dream slipping fast behind him. The dark little girl who had made this mess, this terrible and intolerable mess, was waiting to be sent for in a town in Tennessee.

In fifteen minutes the woman from whom he sublet his room knocked and asked him with maddening kindness if, since he was home, he would have some lunch. He shook his head, but the interruption aroused him, and getting up from the bed he wrote a telegram.

"Letter depressed me have you lost your nerve you are foolish and just upset to think of breaking off why not marry me immediately sure we can make it all right—"

He hesitated for a wild minute, and then added in a hand that could scarcely be recognized as his own: "In any case I will arrive tomorrow at six o'clock."

When he finished he ran out of the apartment and down to the telegraph office near the subway stop. He possessed in this world not quite one hundred dollars, but the letter showed that she was "nervous" and this left him no choice. He knew what "nervous" meant— that she was emotionally depressed, that the prospect of marrying into a life of poverty and struggle was putting too much strain upon her love.

George O'Kelly reached the insurance company at his usual run, the run that had become almost second nature to him, that seemed best to express the tension under which he lived. He went straight to the manager's office.

"I want to see you, Mr. Chambers," he announced breathlessly.

"Well?" Two eyes, eyes like winter windows, glared at him with ruthless impersonality.

"I want to get four days' vacation."

"Why, you had a vacation just two weeks ago!" said Mr. Chambers in surprise.

"That's true," admitted the distraught young man, "but now I've got to have another."

"Where'd you go last time? To your home?"

"No, I went to—a place in Tennessee."

"Well, where do you want to go this time?"

"Well, this time I want to go to—a place in Tennessee."

"You're consistent, anyhow," said the manager dryly. "But I didn't realize you were employed here as a traveling salesman."

"I'm not," cried George desperately, "but I've got to go."

"All right," agreed Mr. Chambers, "but you don't have to come back. So don't!"

"I won't." And to his own astonishment as well as Mr. Chambers', George's face grew pink with pleasure. He felt happy, exultant—for the first time in six months he was absolutely free. Tears of gratitude stood in his eyes, and he seized Mr. Chambers warmly by the hand.

"I want to thank you," he said with a rush of emotion, "I don't want to come back. I think I'd have gone crazy if you'd said that I could come back. Only I couldn't quit myself, you see, and I want to thank you for—for quitting for me."

He waved his hand magnanimously, shouted aloud, "You owe me three days' salary but you can keep it!" and rushed from the office. Mr. Chambers rang for his stenographer to ask if O'Kelly had seemed queer lately. He had fired many men in the course of his career, and they had taken it in many different ways, but none of them had thanked him—ever before.

II

Jonquil Cary was her name, and to George O'Kelly nothing had ever looked so fresh and pale as her face when she saw him and fled to him eagerly along the station platform. Her arms were raised to him, her mouth was half parted for his kiss, when she held him off suddenly and lightly and, with a touch of embarrassment, looked around. Two boys, somewhat younger than George, were standing in the background.

"This is Mr. Craddock and Mr. Holt," she announced cheerfully. "You met them when you were here before."

Disturbed by the transition of a kiss into an introduction and suspecting some hidden significance, George was more confused when he found that the automobile which was to carry them to Jonquil's house belonged to one of the two young men. It seemed to put him at a disadvantage. On the way Jonquil chattered between the front and back seats, and when he tried to slip his arm around her under cover of the twilight she compelled him with a quick movement to take her hand instead.

"Is this street on the way to your house?" he whispered. "I don't recognize it."

"It's the new boulevard. Jerry just got this car today, and he wants to show it to me before he takes us home."

When, after twenty minutes, they were deposited at Jonquil's house, George felt that the first happiness of the meeting, the joy he had recognized so surely in her eyes back in the station, had been dissipated by the intrusion of the ride. Something that he had looked forward to had been rather casually lost, and he was brooding on this as he said good night stiffly to the two young men. Then his ill-humor faded as Jonquil drew him into a familiar embrace under the dim light of the front hall and told him in a dozen ways, of which the best was without words, how she had missed him. Her emotion reassured him, promised his anxious heart that everything would be all right.

They sat together on the sofa, overcome by each other's presence, beyond all except fragmentary endearments. At the supper hour Jonquil's father and mother appeared and were glad to see George. They liked him, and had been interested in his engineering career when he had first come to Tennessee over a year before. They had been sorry when he had given it up and gone to New York to look for something more immediately profitable, but while they deplored the curtailment of his career they sympathized with him and were ready to recognize the engagement. During dinner they asked about his progress in New York.

"Everything's going fine," he told them with enthusiasm. "I've been promoted—better salary."

He was miserable as he said this—but they were all so glad.

"They must like you," said Mrs. Cary, "that's certain—or they wouldn't let you off twice in three weeks to come down here."

"I told them they had to," explained George hastily; "I told them if they didn't I wouldn't work for them any more."

"But you ought to save your money," Mrs. Cary reprached him gently. "Not spend it all on this expensive trip."

Dinner was over—he and Jonquil were alone and she came back into his arms.

"So glad you're here," she sighed. "Wish you never were going away again, darling."

"Do you miss me?"

"Oh, so much, so much."

"Do you—do other men come to see you often? Like those two kids?"

The question surprised her. The dark velvet eyes stared at him.

"Why, of course they do. All the time. Why—I've told you in letters that they did, dearest."

This was true—when he had first come to the city there had been already a dozen boys around her, responding to her picturesque fragility with adolescent worship, and a few of them perceiving that her beautiful eyes were also sane and kind.

"Do you expect me never to go anywhere"—Jonquil demanded, leaning back against the sofa pillows until she seemed to look at him from many miles away—"and just fold my hands and sit still—forever?"

"What do you mean?" he blurted out in a panic. "Do you mean you think I'll never have enough money to marry you?"

"Oh, don't jump at conclusions so, George."

"I'm not jumping at conclusions. That's what you said."

George decided suddenly that he was on dangerous grounds. He had not intended to let anything spoil this night. He tried to take her again in his arms, but she resisted unexpectedly, saying:

"It's hot. I'm going to get the electric fan."

When the fan was adjusted they sat down again, but he was in a supersensitive mood and involuntarily he plunged into the specific world he had intended to avoid.

"When will you marry me?"

"Are you ready for me to marry you?"

All at once his nerves gave way, and he sprang to his feet.

"Let's shut off that damned fan," he cried, "it drives me wild. It's like a clock ticking away all the time I'll be with you. I came here to be happy and forget everything about New York and time—"

He sank down on the sofa as suddenly as he had risen. Jonquil turned off the fan, and drawing his head down into her lap began stroking his hair.

"Let's sit like this," she said softly, "just sit quiet like this, and I'll put you to sleep. You're all tired and nervous and your sweetheart'll take care of you."

"But I don't want to sit like this," he complained, jerking up suddenly, "I don't want to sit like this at all.

I want you to kiss me. That's the only thing that makes me rest. And anyways I'm not nervous—it's you that's nervous. I'm not nervous at all."

To prove that he wasn't nervous he left the couch and plumped himself into a rocking-chair across the room.

"Just when I'm ready to marry you you write me the most nervous letters, as if you're going to back out, and I have to come rushing down here—"

"You don't have to come if you don't want to."

"But I *do* want to!" insisted George.

It seemed to him that he was being very cool and logical and that she was putting him deliberately in the wrong. With every word they were drawing farther and farther apart—and he was unable to stop himself or to keep worry and pain out of his voice.

But in a minute Jonquil began to cry sorrowfully and he came back to the sofa and put his arm around her. He was the comforter now, drawing her head close to his shoulder, murmuring old familiar things until she grew calmer and only trembled a little, spasmodically, in his arms. For over an hour they sat there, while the evening pianos thumped their last cadences into the street outside. George did not move, or think, or hope, lulled into numbness by the premonition of disaster. The clock would tick on, past eleven, past twelve, and then Mrs. Cary could call down gently over the banister—beyond that he saw only tomorrow and despair.

III

In the heat of the next day the breaking-point came. They had each guessed the truth about the other, but of the two she was the more ready to admit the situation.

"There's no use going on," she said miserably, "you know you hate the insurance business, and you'll never do well in it."

"That's not it," he insisted stubbornly; "I hate going on alone. If you'll marry me and come with me and take a chance with me, I can make good at anything, but not while I'm worrying about you down here."

She was silent a long time before she answered, not thinking—for she had seen the end—but only waiting, because she knew that every word would seem more cruel than the last. Finally she spoke:

"George, I love you with all my heart, and I don't see how I can ever love any one else but you. If you'd been ready for me two months ago I'd have married you—now I can't because it doesn't seem to be the sensible thing."

He made wild accusations—there was some one else—she was keeping something from him!

"No, there's no one else."

This was true. But reacting from the strain of this affair she had found relief in the company of young boys like Jerry Holt, who had the merit of meaning absolutely nothing in her life.

George didn't take the situation well, at all. He seized her in his arms and tried literally to kiss her into marrying him at once. When this failed, he broke into a long monologue of self-pity, and ceased only when he saw that he was making himself despicable in her sight. He threatened to leave when he had no intention of leaving, and refused to go when she told him that, after all, it was best that he should.

For a while she was sorry, then for another while she was merely kind.

"You'd better go now," she cried at last, so loud that Mrs. Cary came downstairs in alarm.

"Is something the matter?"

"I'm going away, Mrs. Cary," said George brokenly. Jonquil had left the room.

"Don't feel so badly, George." Mrs. Cary blinked at

him in helpless sympathy—sorry and, in the same breath, glad that the little tragedy was almost done. "If I were you I'd go home to your mother for a week or so. Perhaps after all this is the sensible thing—"

"Please don't talk," he cried. "Please don't say anything to me now!"

Jonquil came into the room again, her sorrow and her nervousness alike tucked under powder and rouge and hat.

"I've ordered a taxicab," she said impersonally. "We can drive around until your train leaves."

She walked out on the front porch. George put on his coat and hat and stood for a minute exhausted in the hall—he had eaten scarcely a bite since he had left New York. Mrs. Cary came over, drew his head down and kissed him on the cheek, and he felt very ridiculous and weak in his knowledge that the scene had been ridiculous and weak at the end. If he had only gone the night before—left her for the last time with a decent pride.

The taxi had come, and for an hour these two that had been lovers rode along the less-frequented streets. He held her hand and grew calmer in the sunshine, seeing too late that there had been nothing all along to do or say.

"I'll come back," he told her.

"I know you will," she answered, trying to put a cheery faith into her voice. "And we'll write each other—sometimes."

"No," he said, "we won't write. I couldn't stand that. Some day I'll come back."

"I'll never forget you, George."

They reached the station, and she went with him while he bought his ticket. . . .

"Why, George O'Kelly and Jonquil Cary!"

It was a man and a girl whom George had known when he had worked in town, and Jonquil seemed to greet their presence with relief. For an interminable five minutes they all stood there talking; then the train roared into the station, and with ill-concealed agony in his face George held out his arms toward Jonquil. She took an uncertain step toward him, faltered, and then pressed his hand quickly as if she were taking leave of a chance friend.

"Good-by, George," she was saying. "I hope you have a pleasant trip.

"Good-by, George. Come back and see us all again."

Dumb, almost blind with pain, he seized his suitcase, and in some dazed way got himself aboard the train.

Past clanging street-crossings, gathering speed through wide suburban spaces toward the sunset. Perhaps she too would see the sunset and pause for a moment, turning, remembering, before he faded with her sleep into the past. This night's dusk would cover up forever the sun and the trees and the flowers and laughter of his young world.

IV

On a damp afternoon in September of the following year a young man with his face burned to a deep copper glow got off a train at a city in Tennessee. He looked around anxiously, and seemed relieved when he found that there was no one in the station to meet him. He taxied to the best hotel in the city where he registered with some satisfaction as George O'Kelly, Cuzco, Peru.

Up in his room he sat for a few minutes at the window looking down into the familiar street below. Then with his hand trembling faintly he took off the telephone receiver and called a number.

"Is Miss Jonquil in?"

"This is she."

"Oh—" His voice after overcoming a faint tendency to waver went on with friendly formality.

"This is George O'Kelly. Did you get my letter?"

"Yes. I thought you'd be in today."

Her voice, cool and unmoved, disturbed him, but not as he had expected. This was the voice of a stranger, unexcited, pleasantly glad to see him—that was all. He wanted to put down the telephone and catch his breath.

"I haven't seen you for—a long time." He succeeded in making this sound offhand. "Over a year."

He knew how long it had been—to the day.

"It'll be awfully nice to talk to you again."

"I'll be there in about an hour."

He hung up. For four long seasons every minute of his leisure had been crowded with anticipation of this hour, and now this hour was here. He had thought of finding her married, engaged, in love—he had not thought she would be unstirred at his return.

There would never again in his life, he felt, be another ten months like these he had just gone through. He had made an admittedly remarkable showing for a young engineer—stumbled into two unusual opportunities, one in Peru, whence he had just returned, and another, consequent upon it, in New York, whither he was bound. In this short time he had risen from poverty into a position of unlimited opportunity.

He looked at himself in the dressing-table mirror. He was almost black with tan, but it was a romantic black, and in the last week, since he had had time to think about it, it had given him considerable pleasure. The hardiness of his frame, too, he appraised with a sort of fascination. He had lost part of an eyebrow somewhere, and he still wore an elastic bandage on his knee, but he was too young not to realize that on the steamer many women had looked at him with unusual tributary interest.

His clothes, of course, were frightful. They had been made for him by a Greek tailor in Lima—in two days. He was young enough, too, to have explained this sartorial deficiency to Jonquil in his otherwise laconic note. The only further detail it contained was a request that he should not be met at the station.

George O'Kelly, of Cuzco, Peru, waited an hour and a half in the hotel, until, to be exact, the sun had reached a midway position in the sky. Then, freshly shaven and talcum-powdered toward a somewhat more Caucasian hue, for vanity at the last minute had overcome romance, he engaged a taxicab and set out for the house he knew so well.

He was breathing hard—he noticed this but he told himself that it was excitement, not emotion. He was here; she was not married—that was enough. He was not even sure what he had to say to her. But this was the moment of his life that he felt he could least easily have dispensed with. There was no triumph, after all, without a girl concerned, and if he did not lay his spoils at her feet he could at least hold them for a passing moment before her eyes.

The house loomed up suddenly beside him, and his first thought was that it had assumed a strange unreality. There was nothing changed—only everything was changed. It was smaller and it seemed shabbier than before—there was no cloud of magic hovering over its roof and issuing from the windows of the upper floor. He rang the doorbell and an unfamiliar maid appeared. Miss Jonquil would be down in a moment. He wet his lips nervously and walked into the sitting-room—and the feeling of unreality increased. After all, he saw, this was only a room, and not the enchanted chamber where he had passed those poignant hours. He sat in a chair, amazed to find it a chair, realizing that his imagination had distorted and colored all these simple familiar things.

Then the door opened and Jonquil came into the room—and it was as though everything in it suddenly blurred before his eyes. He had not remembered how beautiful she was, and he felt his face grow pale and his voice diminish to a poor sigh in his throat.

She was dressed in pale green, and a gold ribbon bound back her dark, straight hair like a crown. The familiar velvet eyes caught his as she came through the door, and a spasm of fright went through him at her beauty's power of inflicting pain.

He said "Hello," and they each took a few steps forward and shook hands. Then they sat in chairs quite far apart and gazed at each other across the room.

"You've come back," she said, and he answered just as tritely: "I wanted to stop in and see you as I came through."

He tried to neutralize the tremor in his voice by looking anywhere but at her face. The obligation to speak was on him, but, unless he immediately began to boast, it seemed that there was nothing to say. There had never been anything casual in their previous relations—it didn't seem possible that people in this position would talk about the weather.

"This is ridiculous," he broke out in sudden embarrassment. "I don't know exactly what to do. Does my being here bother you?"

"No." The answer was both reticent and impersonally sad. It depressed him.

"Are you engaged?" he demanded.

"No."

"Are you in love with some one?"

She shook her head.

"Oh." He leaned back in his chair. Another subject seemed exhausted—the interview was not taking the course he had intended.

"Jonquil," he began, this time on a softer key, "after all that's happened between us, I wanted to come back and see you. Whatever I do in the future I'll never love another girl as I've loved you."

This was one of the speeches he had rehearsed. On the steamer it had seemed to have just the right note—a reference to the tenderness he would always feel for her combined with a non-committal attitude toward his present state of mind. Here with the past around him, beside him, growing minute by minute more heavy on the air, it seemed theatrical and stale.

She made no comment, sat without moving, her eyes fixed on him with an expression that might have meant everything or nothing.

"You don't love me any more, do you?" he asked her in a level voice.

"No."

When Mrs. Cary came in a minute later, and spoke to him about his success—there had been a half-column about him in the local paper—he was a mixture of emotions. He knew now that he still wanted this girl, and he knew that the past sometimes comes back—that was all. For the rest he must be strong and watchful and he would see.

"And now," Mrs. Cary was saying, "I want you two to go and see the lady who has the chrysanthemums. She particularly told me she wanted to see you because she'd read about you in the paper."

They went to see the lady with the chrysanthemums. They walked along the street, and he recognized with a sort of excitement just how her shorter footsteps always fell in between his own. The lady turned out to be nice, and the chrysanthemums were enormous and extraordinarily beautiful. The lady's gardens were full of them, white and pink and yellow, so that to be among them was a trip back into the heart of summer. There were two gardens full, and a gate between them; when they strolled toward the second garden the lady went first through the gate.

And then a curious thing happened. George stepped aside to let Jonquil pass, but instead of going through she stood still and stared at him for a minute. It was not so much the look, which was not a smile, as it was the moment of silence. They saw each other's eyes, and both took a short, faintly accelerated breath, and then they went on into the second garden. That was all.

The afternoon waned. They thanked the lady and walked home slowly, thoughtfully, side by side. Through dinner, too, they were silent. George told Mr. Cary something of what had happened in South America, and managed to let it be known that everything would be plain sailing for him in the future.

Then dinner was over, and he and Jonquil were alone in the room which had seen the beginning of their love affair and the end. It seemed to him long ago and inexpressibly sad. On that sofa he had felt agony and grief such as he would never feel again. He would never be so weak or so tired and miserable and poor. Yet he knew that that boy of fifteen months before had had something, a trust, a warmth that was gone forever. The sensible thing—they had done the sensible thing. He had traded his first youth for strength and carved success out of despair. But with his youth, life had carried away the freshness of his love.

"You won't marry me, will you?" he said quietly.

Jonquil shook her dark head.

"I'm never going to marry," she answered.

He nodded.

"I'm going on to Washington in the morning," he said.

"Oh—"

"I have to go. I've got to be in New York by the first, and meanwhile I want to stop off in Washington."

"Business!"

"No-o," he said as if reluctantly. "There's some one there I must see who was very kind to me when I was so—down and out."

This was invented. There was no one in Washington for him to see—but he was watching Jonquil narrowly, and he was sure that she winced a little, that her eyes closed and then opened wide again.

"But before I go I want to tell you the things that happened to me since I saw you, and, as maybe we won't meet again, I wonder if—if just this once you'd sit in my lap like you used to. I wouldn't ask except since there's no one else—yet—perhaps it doesn't matter."

She nodded, and in a moment was sitting in his lap as she had sat so often in that vanished spring. The feel of her head against his shoulder, of her familiar body, sent a shock of emotion over him. His arms holding her had a tendency to tighten around her, so he leaned back and began to talk thoughtfully into the air.

He told her of a despairing two weeks in New York which had terminated with an attractive if not very profitable job in a construction plant in Jersey City. When the Peru business had first presented itself it had not seemed an extraordinary opportunity. He was to be third assistant engineer on the expedition, but only ten of the American party, including eight rodmen and surveyors, had ever reached Cuzco. Ten days later the chief of the expedition was dead of yellow fever. That had been his chance, a chance for anybody but a fool, a marvellous chance—

"A chance for anybody but a fool?" she interrupted innocently.

"Even for a fool," he continued. "It was wonderful. Well, I wired New York—"

"And so," she interrupted again, "they wired that you ought to take a chance?"

"Ought to!" he exclaimed, still leaning back. "That I *had* to. There was no time to lose—"

"Not a minute?"

"Not a minute."

"Not even time for—" she paused.

"For what?"

"Look."

He bent his head forward suddenly, and she drew herself to him in the same moment, her lips half open like a flower.

"Yes," he whispered into her lips. "There's all the time in the world . . ."

All the time in the world—his life and hers. But for an instant as he kissed her he knew that though he search through eternity he could never recapture those lost April hours. He might press her close now till the muscles knotted on his arms—she was something desirable and rare that he had fought for and made his own—but never again an intangible whisper in the dusk, or on the breeze of night. . . .

Well, let it pass, he thought; April is over, April is over. There are all kinds of love in the world, but never the same love twice.

from Love and Marriage

by Bill Cosby

At the beginning of Act Five, Shakespeare's Theseus finds similarity between the lunatic and the lover. According to contemporary humorist Bill Cosby, Shakespeare "was wrong: the lunatic had more sense" than the lover, as we see with the adolescent Bill Cosby who schemed to take revenge on the girl who "dumped" him. Here, Cosby tells the fanciful story of his mission to punish Charlene Gibson, once the girl of his dreams.

During my last year of high school, I fell in love so hard with a girl that it made my love for Sarah McKinney seem like a stupid infatuation with a teacher. Charlene Gibson was the Real Thing and she would be Mrs. Charlene Cosby, serving me hot dogs and watching me drive to the hoop and giving me the full-court press for the rest of my life.

In tribute to our great love, I was moved to give Charlene something to wear. A Temple T-shirt didn't seem quite right and neither did my Truman button. What Charlene needed was a piece of jewelry; and I was able to find the perfect one, an elegant pin, in my mother's dresser drawer.

Ten days after I had made this grand presentation, Charlene dumped me; but, sentimentalist that she was, she kept the pin. When I confessed my dark deed to my mother, she didn't throw a brick at me, she merely wanted to have the pin back, a request that I felt was not unreasonable since I had stolen it.

Moreover, retrieving the pin was important to me, but for a romantic reason: I wanted to punish Charlene. Paying back the person with whom you have recently been in love is one of life's most precious moments.

"I want that pin back," I said to Charlene on the phone.

"I can't do that," she replied.

"Why not?"

"Because I lost it."

"You *lost* it?"

"That's what I just said."

"How could you *lose* it?"

"Easy. First I had it, then I didn't."

And so, I went to her house, where her mother said she wasn't home. Nervously I told her mother why I needed the pin returned and she understood without saying I had done anything wrong. Of course, she didn't have the world's sharpest judgment because she still thought I was a wonderful person. In fact, all the mothers of the girls who rejected me thought I was a wonderful person; I would have made a fine father to those girls.

"Mrs. Gibson," I said, "Charlene told me she lost the pin. I'm not saying I don't believe her, but I don't."

"Just one minute, William," she said, and she turned and went upstairs. Moments later, she returned with the pin. And then I went home and waited for the satisfaction of Charlene calling me to say:

How dare *you go to my house and ask my mother for that pin!*

But no call from her came.

Probably because she's ashamed of lying to me, I told myself; *but maybe because she truly likes me and wants to keep the pin for that reason.*

I was convincing myself that Charlene wanted to have an elegant token of me and that now I should call *her* to rekindle this wondrous love-hate relationship, for Charlene and I had been meant for each other: she was a liar and I was a thief. Two such people, who had been so deeply in love, should have had a chance to keep torturing each other. We once had kissed for almost three hours, inhaling each other and talking about how many children we should have. True, she was the kind of girl who might be having children by other men too, but there was still a softness about her I liked, a softness that matched the one in my head. We had been too close for our relationship to end with her dumping me. We had to get back together so I could dump *her.*

All these thoughts went through my head as I sat with my hand on the phone, wanting to get into a fight with Charlene for old times' sake. Shakespeare said that the lunatic and the lover are the same, but he was wrong: the lunatic has more sense than the man who wanted to call Charlene so that he could hang up on her. However, I had to be very careful to keep her from hanging up on *me* or else she would have been two ahead of me, with no overtime to play.

Finally, after the kind of reasoning that made Napoleon invade Russia, I picked up the phone.

"Hello, Charlene," I said, at least beginning well by getting her name right.

"Yes," she coldly replied, neatly falling into my trap.

"I think you owe me an apology."

"Oh, is that what you think?"

"It certainly is."

Note how cleverly I was preparing her for the kill.

"So that's the way you feel?" I said. "That no apology is necessary?"

"That's the way I feel; I just said it. You have some problem with English?"

"No, I'm just checking to see if you really want to keep the reputation of being a dishonest person and lying about having something that belonged to somebody else."

"You stole the pin from your mother and you're calling *me* dishonest?"

"But you didn't *know* I stole it. And it meant something special to me."

"I didn't *ask* you to give it to me," she said.

"But you *lied* about losing it."

"No, I didn't. I didn't know where it was."

"Your mother went right upstairs and found it."

"Just the way *you* found it in your mother's drawer."

My appetite for humiliation was clearly boundless as I pressed on in a conversation that revealed new dimensions in male dumbness.

"Put your mother on the phone," I said.

"Put *your* mother on the phone," she said, "and I'll ask her how it feels to have a crazy son."

"Crazy, huh? It just so happens that I was crazy in love with you. Have you already forgotten our plans to have children?"

"Well, start without me. I'm definitely not having them if they're yours."

"And that's just fine with me."

"Me too."

"Look, Charlene . . . I don't think we should end this by being angry with each other."

"Yeah, I guess not."

"I know that you're in love with someone else this week and I wish you the best."

"Coming from you, that means nothing to me."

"Look, Charlene, I think we should end this by being friends. I think we should end it so . . . well, so if you ever want to call me and ask me a question, like how to break a zone defense or something, I'll be happy to give you the answer."

Now note how cleverly I was luring her into a

position where I could dump her last and make her feel sorry she had ever known me, a sentiment she already may have felt.

"I don't think I'll be calling you," she said.

"So that's the way you feel?"

"Why do I have to tell you everything twice? I think I've told you enough."

And then she hung up. She hadn't even said good-bye—once.

Should I call her back to slam her with my own good-bye? I asked myself.

No, I decided. I would find the revenge that she deserved for messing around with my heart, the only part of my body that I could never get into shape.

The revenge I devised had a simple splendor: I would find a girl who was prettier than Charlene, entice her into a relationship, and then flaunt this relationship to Charlene, who would promptly jump off a cliff. And so, with both the dedication and the mental balance of Captain Ahab chasing Moby Dick, I began my great hunt. The following day, I began pursuing a gorgeous girl I'll call Artemis, after the Greek Goddess of Virginity. For many months, boys had been throwing themselves at Artemis like tacklers trying to bring down Jim Brown. Nonetheless, on this day, I summoned the courage to approach her and say, "Hi, I'm Bill Cosby and I was wondering if you're going to John Thomas's party on Friday night."

She looked at me silently for a moment, but I knew that she knew who I was because I had played varsity basketball on nights when the girls had come out of hiding.

"No, I'm not going," she said.

And suddenly I feared that her refusal to go with me would get back to Charlene and make her heart sing.

"But we've been talking about going, haven't we?" said one of several girls who made up Artemis' entourage.

Fixing me with a cool look, she said, "What time's the party?"

"Eight o'clock," I replied.

"Okay, I'll go with you."

"Yeah, we'll go with you," said one of her friends.

"Right, we'll go," said a third.

"Could I talk to you alone for a minute?" I said to Artemis.

"I guess so," she said, clearly falling for me.

Taking her hand, I led her away from the entourage and said, "Look, I want to go to the party with *you,* not a field hockey team."

"They're my friends."

"And I'm glad you have them. But can't you give them a night off and go just with *me?*"

"I thought you were going steady with Charlene."

"Yeah, I was, but *she* wasn't, so I released her. And a lucky thing too 'cause it made room for you. Listen, you want to come and watch track practice this afternoon?"

"Not really."

"I do the high jump."

"I'm sure you do."

"And I'll be jumping just for you."

"The way you jumped for Charlene?"

"Charlene was just a high hurdle compared to you."

And not sounding like an idiot was a high hurdle for me too, but this divine female was heady stuff.

"Okay, then," she said, "you'll pick me up on Friday around eight?"

"You bet," I said, wondering how I was going to pick her up in a trolley.

When Friday came, however, I was able to pick her up in a car driven by my friend Ed Ford, who'd agreed to double date because he couldn't believe that Artemis had fallen off her pedestal and into the depths occupied by me.

"I still don't see her going with *you*," said Ed as we drove to her house. "Maybe she's gonna become a nun and has to do some kinda suffering."

"You just don't understand women," I said. "She *knows* I'm using her to pay back Charlene, and she's doing it 'cause women hate each other. But the funny thing is, I'm also falling in love with her."

"And when she dumps you, who you gonna use to punish *her?*" said Ed. "Lena Horne? Man, you're over your head in beauty."

But he was wrong: I had *lost* my head in beauty, so the Friday party became a blend of revenge and desire for me. A few minutes after Artemis and I had arrived, while I was busy parading her like a poodle going for Best in Show, Charlene came in—and suddenly, my future and past were together in one room. Charlene saw me with Artemis, of course, and I was delighted that her suffering had begun. Putting my face close to Artemis' face, I broke into laughter, as if she had just said something hilarious.

"You feelin' okay?" she said.

"Never better," I told her, still laughing.

"You been hittin' that high bar a lot?"

"I love it when you talk like that."

A few seconds later, seeing Charlene move to the punch bowl, I said to Artemis, "Will you excuse me for a moment?"

"For as long as you want," she replied.

I turned and walked over to Charlene, casually saying, "Why, Charlene Gibson, I *thought* it was you. What're *you* doing here?"

"Making a big mistake," she said. "Artemis and

you? Since when did she start doing social work with thieves?"

"Glad you're having fun, Charlene."

"What're you gonna steal for *her?* Your mother's *watch?*"

"Have some pink and white mints. They'll really clear your head."

"I know you, Bill Cosby. You're just rentin' that girl to make me feel bad. I thought you wanted to be friends."

"Well, I did," I said, suddenly wishing that I had chosen a more gracious revenge.

"I thought you wanted me to be able to ask you questions."

"Well . . . yeah."

"Okay, here's one: Are you ever gonna grow up?"

It was a simple true-false question, the kind on which I usually guessed, and so I took a guess now: "I certainly am."

Often through the years, I have thought of Charlene's question; and I now know the answer is that no man ever grows up in the eyes of a woman— or ever grows familiar with the rules for dealing with her. Sigmund Freud once said, "What do women want?" The only thing I have learned in fifty-two years is that women want men to stop asking dumb questions like that.

Acknowledgments

(continued from page ii)

HarperCollins Publishers, Inc.: Excerpt from "Love's Initiations," from *Care of the Soul* by Thomas Moore. Copyright © 1992 by Thomas Moore. Reprinted by permission of HarperCollins Publishers, Inc.

Simon & Schuster, Inc.: "The Sensible Thing" by F. Scott Fitzgerald. Reprinted with permission of Scribner, a division of Simon & Schuster, from *The Short Stories of F. Scott Fitzgerald*, edited by Matthew J. Bruccoli. Copyright 1924 by Coloroto Corporation. Copyright renewed 1952 by Frances Scott Fitzgerald Lanahan.

Doubleday: Excerpt from *Love & Marriage* by Bill Cosby. Copyright © 1989 by Bill Cosby. Used by permission of Doubleday, a division of Bantam Doubleday Dell Publishing Group, Inc.